Gentles and ladymen, are you sick and tired of making the same baking recipes again and again? Then look no further than this baking blast from the past, as B. Dylan Hollis highlights the most unique tasty treats of yesteryear. You'll travel back on a delicious decade-by-decade jaunt as Dylan shows you how to bake the vintage forgotten greats—everything from Chocolate Potato Cake from the 1910s to Avocado Pie from the 1960s.

Dylan has baked hundreds of recipes from countless antique cookbooks and selected only the best for this bakebook, sharing the shining stars from each decade. And because some of the recipes Dylan shares on his wildly popular social media channels are spectacular failures, he's thrown in a few of the most disastrously strange recipes for you to try if you dare.

Baking Yesteryear contains 101 expertly curated recipes that will take you on a delicious journey through the past. With a larger-than-life personality and comedic puns galore, baking with Dylan never gets old. We'll leave that to the recipes.

BAKING
YESTERYEAR

BAKING YESTERYEAR

the best recipes from the 1900s to the 1980s

B. DYLAN HOLLIS

Publisher Mike Sanders
Senior Editor Alexander Rigby
Art & Design Director William Thomas
Lifestyle Photography Lauren Jones
Styling Assistant Emma Chance
Food Photography Kelley Jordan Schuyler
Food Stylist Lovoni Walker
Recipe Tester Jordan DeFigio
Compositor Ayanna Lacey
Proofreaders Megan Douglass, Lisa Himes
Indexer Celia McCoy

First American Edition, 2023
Published in the United States by DK Publishing
6081 E. 82nd Street, Indianapolis, IN 46250

The authorized representative in the EEA is Dorling Kindersley
Verlag GmbH. Arnulfstr. 124, 80636 Munich, Germany

Copyright © 2023 B. Dylan Hollis
23 24 25 26 27 10 9 8 7 6 5 4 3 2
002-335525-JUL2023

Library of Congress Catalog Number: 2022950526
ISBN 978-0-7440-8004-9

DK books are available at special discounts when purchased in bulk
for sales promotions, premiums, fund-raising, or educational use.
For details, contact: SpecialSales@dk.com

Printed and bound in China

For the curious
www.dk.com

MIX
Paper | Supporting
responsible forestry
FSC™ C018179
www.fsc.org

This book was made with Forest
Stewardship Council ™ certified
paper – one small step in DK's
commitment to a sustainable future.
For more information go to
www.dk.com/our-green-pledge

To my Granny, Peggy Hollis

Contents

11   Introduction

27   1900s

47   1910s

67   1920s

85   Dates

97   1930s

117   1940s

137   1950s

157   No-Bake

171   1960s

191   1970s

213   1980s

233   Worst of the Worst

245   Conclusion

1900s

Pecan Dainties.............................. 28
Cornflake Macaroons........................31
Food for the Gods.......................... 32
Cream Spice Cake.......................... 35
Sandtorte 36
Election Cake 39
Pioneer Brownies 40
Hot Cross Buns.............................43
Hermits 45

1910s

Starchies..................................... 49
Pork Cake 50
Admiral's Gingerbread......................53
Chocolate Potato Cake 54
The Lady Baltimore 57
ANZAC Biscuits............................ 58
Rice Pudding.................................59
Carrot Pie................................... 62
Divinity 65

1920s

Ricciarelli 69
Hedgehogs...................................70
Maple-Squash Gems 72
Poorman's Pie 73
Dutch Apple Cake 74
Blackberry Jam Cake 77
Continental Johnny Cake 78
Unemployment Pudding....................81
Anadama Bread 82

Dates

Date Soufflé................................. 87
Date Bars 88
Date Macaroons 93
Date Nut Loaf 94

1930s

Icebox Pinwheels 99
Rocks...100
Peanut Butter Bread 103
Wacky Cake.................................104
Whipped Cream Cake 107
Mock Apple Pie 108
Potato Doughnuts 111
Baked Apples 112
Potato Candy............................... 113
Banana Marlow..............................115

1940s

Peanut Butter Styrofoams...................119
Dream Bars 120
Oatmeal Honey Bread......................123
Leftover Bread Pancakes 126
Sour Cream Cookies 127
Chocolate Sauerkraut Cake................128
Applesauce Graham Cracker Torte.....131
Queen of Puddings 132
Peppermint Patties 135

1950s

Melting Moments 139
Tomato Soup Cake 140
Color Vision Cake 143
Boiled Cookies 144
Forgotten Cookies 145
Chocolate Mayonnaise Cake 147
Valentine's Cream Pie 148
Kiskadee Fantasy 151
Cocomalt Cheesecake 152
Cereal Crunch Nougat Bars 153
Cathedral Cookies 155

No-Bake

Liquor Balls 159
Candle Salad 160
Penguin Icebox Cake 162
Magic Ice Cream 163
Coconut Ice 167
Ambrosia 168

1960s

Cowboy Cookies 173
Double Chocolate Potato Drops 174
Haystacks 177
Midnight Mallowmalt Cake 178
Grasshopper Pie 181
Lemon Sponge 182
Hello Dollies 183
Millionaire's Pie 185
Avocado Pie 186
Scotcheroos 189

1970s

Potato Chip Cookies 193
Ice Cream Cone Cupcakes 194
Cold Oven Cake 197
Jell-O Poke Cake 201
PB King 202
The Robert Redford 205
Banana Oatmeal Cookies 206
Impossible Pie 207
Deep Fried Cookie Dough 209
Christmas Crack 210

1980s

Monster Cookies 215
Magic Peanut Butter Cookies 216
Banana Split Bars 219
Millionaire's Shortbread 220
Watergate Cake 223
Cream Banana Cake 224
The Buster 227
PB&J Cheesecake 228
Velveeta Fudge 231

Worst of the Worst

Jellied Meatloaf 235
SpaghettiOs Jell-O Ring 236
Roughage Loaf 238
Prune Whip Pie 239
Pickle Cheesecake 240

Introduction

This book is my love letter to the experience of baking yesteryear. It is a collection of the most peculiar recipes that shone their way through the pages of hundreds of old, well-worn cookbooks. They embody my own philosophy of what makes life worth living: the wild, the wacky, and the wonderful. Every recipe herein will contain one, if not all three, of those descriptors. The bakes in this book are not the foremost in perfect, gourmet cooking. Rather, they are the ancestors of humble classics, the ingenious personal curios of home bakers, and the collections of unconventional family recipes from the average kitchens of those rosy days of old.

All of these bakes were derived from countless community cookbooks from the United States, the United Kingdom, and Bermuda. Distinctive personal creations born of church lady committees, parent teacher associations, bridge clubs, and knitting circles, from a time long since forgotten. It is my belief that the curious joys of baking can just as easily emanate from the everyday home baker's imagination, as it can from the staunch and perfectionist kitchen elite.

Baking Yesteryear is for those who want to walk on the sweet side of the street less traveled. To combine ingredients you had never even thought to consider, with the goal of making something once buried by time, but well worth resurrecting. I wanted this book to offer variety in a very different sense, by providing a time machine that is not only edible, but entirely delectable—and I think you'll find just that.

My Story

I have forever been a lover of the old world. My childhood years on the island of Bermuda were spent collecting bygone trinkets, vintage tube radios, records, and mementos from the old grand hotels of my country: a nation renowned for entertaining midcentury tourists with calypso and big band jazz. My life goal has always been to become an entertainer, and having played piano from the age of six, I had resolved to make this a reality, one day aiming to have a nightly jazz set in a hotel ballroom or nightclub.

Coming to the United States in 2014, I continued my music studies by enrolling at the University of Wyoming, where my adoration for yesteryear had me purchase a 1963 Cadillac Series 6200—the same daily driver that you see featured throughout this book—as one of my first steps to living the life I wanted to lead. I was an unusual sight during the morning scrambles to the parking lots. Some toothpick-looking foreigner pulling up in a chromed car the size of a shipping container, walking into the fine arts program to jazz band rehearsal. Utterly inconspicuous.

Now, the only logical next step for a musician is to become a baker. It's well known that a degree in music is a degree in unemployment. But the truth is that I fell into the baking realm with the grace of tripping headfirst into a loaded dishwasher. During my studies (I had decided to fast-track my 4-year degree by condensing it into 8), the COVID-19 pandemic saw the university shutter its doors, and rehearsals and classes went online. Confined to my home, with nobody to speak to but my furniture, I, like many, gravitated toward the new short-format video platform TikTok in the spring of 2020. Between the many trends, I attempted comedy, and uploaded other videos that had nothing to do with baking. I decided to reach for one of the many vintage trinkets I was so used to collecting: an old cookbook. And so on August 29, 2020, I uploaded my first baking video: *Pork Cake*.

Despite knowing naught about baking, cooking, or the kitchen, it seemed to strike a chord with people. The video skyrocketed with views and requests for more, and so I found myself looking for other old cookbooks in antique stores and yard sales. Suddenly I was thumbing through tens of dusty tomes on cookery, baking my way through them, and taste-testing them on camera. People were enthusiastically enthralled by this formula, and I was dumbfounded as to why. Cooking on the internet was supposed to be for the well-versed, featuring fancy, beautiful, photogenic pieces of the sort that make you want to pause and upload a picture before you dig in. Not some skinny git yelling in his college apartment kitchen with bizarre and revolting dishes dead people ate.

Before long, I had millions of loving people behind me, hundreds of cookbooks sent to my post office box, news interviews, television spots, and strangers stopping me at the grocery store to tell me how much I inspired them to start baking. It was unreal. I've often said I'm perhaps one of the only well-known food creators on the internet who hasn't a clue what he's doing. But by experiencing history through the lens of ingredient lists and eating cake, I began to find there was something uniquely fulfilling about it all. For it is one thing to read about the past in nonfiction, to view the past through films, or learn about it in lectures, but to be able to prepare, bake, and taste history is something very, very special indeed.

How to Use This Book

Despite the historical perspective, this cookbook is like any other, in that I will very much tell you what you need to bake things! However, if you are not a baker, there are some terms you might want to familiarize yourself with. Below are words that you will find throughout the book.

CREAM

Used when initially mixing together butter and sugar. In all cases, your butter should be at room temperature, and to cream is to vigorously mix your sugar into your butter. This can be done with a simple wooden spoon, or with a stand mixer or electric hand mixer. The goal is to create a fluffy, light paste, in which all the sugar has been thoroughly incorporated into the butter to create an airy, smooth mixture. This should take some time, about 5 minutes by hand. It is a step that should never be skipped.

BEAT

To beat a mixture is to simply mix it as if you are angry at it. Use force and rigor to combine the ingredients with your spoon exceptionally well. When the term is used for egg whites, use a whisk to thoroughly aerate the mixture into a fluffy, glossy meringue.

FOLD

Folding is the gentler side of mixing by use of a spatula. Folding in ingredients means to cut them into a mixture with the narrow edge of your utensil. Start by vertically "slicing" the ingredient to be folded toward the bottom of the bowl, sliding crosswise, and then up the nearest side. Rotate the bowl slightly and repeat. The goal is to incorporate the ingredient with as little disturbance as possible, so that air is not deflated, or a mixture is not agitated as much as standard mixing.

DOUBLE BOILER

For the purposes of this book, a double boiler is a heatproof bowl set within a larger pot or saucepan of typically simmering, not boiling, water. The bowl's bottom should not touch the water, but instead be heated only by its rising steam. Double boilers are used to melt or heat ingredients that should not come into contact with direct heat.

PEAKS

When beating egg whites or whipping cream, the more you whisk the firmer the mixture becomes, and knowing when to stop is key. In both instances, a whisk attachment should be used, preferably via a stand mixer or the beaters of a handheld mixer.

Soft peaks: The mixture can barely hold its shape when the whisk is removed and its "peak" flops over as you inspect it. It is not liquid, but it is certainly flaccid.

Stiff peaks: The mixture stands erect when the whisk is removed, and its "peak" does not curl nor flop; even when the whisk is moved around.

If egg whites are beaten beyond stiff, the mixture will turn dry and foamy. If cream is whipped beyond stiff, it will turn clumpy and dense. It is worth noting that the time between soft peaks, stiff, and overwhipped cream can be tiny, so go at it slowly. Egg white mixtures are far more forgiving.

Utensils to Have in Your Kitchen

MIXING BOWLS

One should have at least three large mixing bowls, preferably heatproof. Many recipes make use of mixing a variety of ingredients together separately, most often dry and wet. Having multiple bowls makes this easier.

A WOODEN SPOON, A RUBBER SPATULA, & A WHISK

The wooden spoon is my favorite utensil, it is your most eager ally and is of utmost importance for mixing and beating. The spatula is important for folding, and to properly scoop out the entirety of mixtures from bowls into other bowls or baking pans. A whisk is important for the beating or whisking of liquid mixtures.

MEASURING CUPS & SPOONS, KITCHEN SCALE

A collection of ¼ cup, ⅓ cup, ½ cup, and 1 cup measures is essential, so is a ¼ teaspoon, ½ teaspoon, 1 teaspoon, and 1 tablespoon set of measuring spoons. If you're a fan of baking by weight, a scale is also a key tool to have.

A STAND MIXER OR ELECTRIC HAND MIXER

When dealing with beating egg whites, whipping cream, or creating frostings, whisking and beating by hand is possible, but it takes an impressive amount of time and a lot of physical effort. Having a stand mixer or electric hand mixer makes this process a cinch, and will save you much blood, sweat, and tears.

THERMOMETER

Precise temperatures are critical when dealing with certain recipes. Having an instant-read thermometer rated to 300°F (148°C) or a candy thermometer is required for a few of the recipes in this book.

POTS, SAUCEPANS, & SKILLETS

Having at least one 3-quart (2.8 liter) saucepan, and one 8-inch (20cm) skillet or frying pan will come in handy.

PARCHMENT PAPER

I find a roll of parchment paper essential in baking. When used on your cookie sheet, it prevents sticking and allows for easy cleanup. A few recipes also call for its use in the bottom of a baking pan, or as a sling. In this way, baked goods can be removed without sticking. A sling has two ends of the parchment exceeding the pan, allowing them to be grasped, and the baked goods removed effortlessly.

A SIEVE

A few of the recipes use a sieve to sift dry ingredients. This is important to avoid clumping, or to add lightness into mixtures.

BAKEWARE

The majority of recipes in this book make use of 9-inch (23-cm) cake pans; 9-inch (23-cm) pie pans; and 9×9-, 8×8-, and 9×13-inch (23×23-, 20×20-, and 23×33-cm) square and rectangular cake pans. We will also use 10-inch (25-cm) tube and Bundt pans, a 9×5-inch (23×13-cm) loaf pan, and a full-size 21×16-inch (53×40-cm) cookie sheet or baking sheet.

COOKIE SCOOP

I recommend a standard, run-of-the-mill cookie scoop. I use a #60 cookie scoop, which is just over one tablespoon. When a recipe calls for the dropping of dough "by rounded tablespoon" or "by level tablespoon," roughly dollop from, and level the scoop, respectively.

Ingredients

Understanding what foodstuffs you'll need in the kitchen to bake from this book can be done by skimming through the ingredients list of each recipe. However, there are certain mainstays you should have for any baking adventure.

BUTTER

This is the king of baking ingredients. Having a few cups of butter in your fridge is essential. For the purposes of this book, all butter is assumed to be salted unless noted otherwise. However, you do not need to go out and buy salted butter if you're a user of unsalted; it will not change the result of your baking to any appreciable degree. The use of salted butter when unsalted butter is expressly called for (such as in buttercream frostings) is not advised. Butter called for in the recipes is also assumed to be at room temperature, unless noted otherwise.

EGGS

Having a dozen pasteurized eggs (or *eggies!* as I like to say) at the ready is a good move. Medium, large, or extra large will work just fine.

FLOUR

This book uses all-purpose flour as its standard flour variety. Not self-rising nor self-raising. Any other variety will be expressly noted. As it concerns weight, this book takes a slightly liberal designation of 140 grams per cup.

SUGAR, BROWN SUGAR, & POWDERED SUGAR

What use are desserts without sweetness? Having granulated sugar, brown sugar, and powdered sugar (sometimes called icing sugar or confectioner's sugar) will be of use as they appear quite often in this book.

BAKING POWDER & BAKING SODA

These are your primary leavening agents, or *floofers*, as I call them, and they're as crucial for baking as they are for this book. Their job is to make your bakes rise and become fluffy, as opposed to dense and stodgy. They need to be within their expiry window lest they become inactive. You should always be very precise in their measurements by leveling off the measuring spoon with a knife, as even just a little bit too much or too little can cause your baked goods to fail. It is also important that you never confuse baking powder for baking soda, or vice versa.

MILK

Ah yes, the *moo juice*! All milk in this book is whole milk (not 2%, skim, or plant-based). Scalded milk is heated milk brought just below boiling.

SALT

You may not think it, but salt is just as important in desserts and cakes as sugar! Not only does it augment flavor and sweetness, it affects the crumb and texture of bakes, too. Salt will be called for in almost every recipe in this book, so be sure to have some. I recommend table salt or kosher salt, as some sea salts, rock salts, or Himalayan salts can have very large grains which can lead to under measuring.

My Favorites

Although each recipe that has found its way into *Baking Yesteryear* is an absolute darling to me, I have a few to note in particular for their taste or unconventional elegance.

The 1900s
Food for the Gods (page 32)

The 1910s
Chocolate Potato Cake (page 54)

The 1920s
Ricciarelli (page 69)

The 1930s
Whipped Cream Cake (page 107)

The 1940s
Applesauce Graham Cracker Torte (page 131)

The 1950s
Kiskadee Fantasy (page 151)

The 1960s
Haystacks (page 177)

The 1970s
Christmas Crack (page 210)

The 1980s
The Buster (page 227)

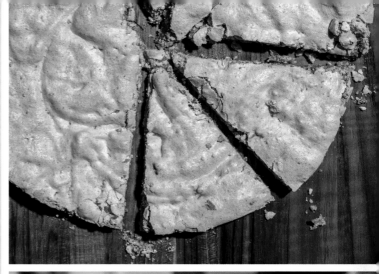

Pie Crust

Single crust for 9-inch pie

1⅓ cups (185g) all-purpose flour

Pinch of salt

½ cup (115g) butter or vegetable
shortening, cold and cubed

4–6 tbsp cold water

Double crust for 9-inch pie

2⅓ cups (325g) all-purpose flour

¾ tsp salt

1 cup (225g) butter or vegetable
shortening, cold and cubed

6–8 tbsp cold water

There will be pies in this book (I sure hope so) that call for a prepared pastry as part of their greater recipe. And while I feel that this buttery, flaky pastry deserves the right to be featured multiple times alongside them, its recipe will instead wait for you here with eagerness.

METHOD

1. Combine the flour and salt into a large bowl. Using a pastry cutter or two knives, cut half of the butter into the flour until the mixture is uniform. Then, add the remaining butter and repeat until the largest pieces are the size of peppercorns. Add water and mix until the dough forms a ball. If the mixture does not hold its shape when squeezed in the hand, additional water may be added. Form a disk of dough resembling a hockey puck (for double crust, divide and form two disks), wrap in plastic wrap, and chill for at least 30 minutes.

2. Turn the disk onto a lightly floured board, and with a floured rolling pin, roll out from the center of the dough to form a circle that extends at least 2 inches (5cm) beyond the rim of your pie pan. While rolling the disk of dough, turn occasionally and lightly flour beneath to prevent sticking. This step will be repeated should you need a double crust pastry.

3. Once the size is adequate, fold the dough gently in half over your rolling pin and center into the pie pan before patting into place to form the bottom crust. Trim the edges evenly, leaving roughly a 1-inch (2.5-cm) overhang beyond the rim. For a single-crust pastry, the overhang may be gently folded over the edge of the pie pan, or it may be fluted or crimped. A simple crimp would be to gently press the tines of a fork into the dough to seal it to the edge of the pie pan.

Vanilla Buttercream Frosting

2 cups (450g) unsalted butter, softened

6 cups (720g) powdered sugar

2 tsp vanilla extract

1–3 tbsp whole milk, if needed to thin

Some of the frostings in this book are quite tricky to manage. Such is the case with the boiled frostings, which you will encounter later on. Should you want to avoid the hassle of thermometers and boiling hot syrups, this lusciously smooth American buttercream frosting is a fine alternative. It may not be historically appropriate for some of the cakes in the book, but that doesn't mean it won't taste fantastic.

METHOD

1. In the bowl of a stand mixer fitted with a paddle attachment, or a large bowl with which an electric hand mixer is to be used, beat the butter on high speed until it lightens. About 3 minutes.

2. Reducing the mixer speed to medium-high, gradually beat in the powdered sugar 2 tablespoons at a time with the mixer running. Mix in the vanilla.

3. Increase the mixer speed to high, and beat until pale, creamy, and uniform. About 5 minutes. If the mixture is too stiff to spread/pipe, milk may be beaten in.

4. To frost your cake, first ensure the cake has cooled completely. Then place it on a suitable surface (such as a cake stand or a turntable), and spread a generous amount of frosting evenly atop the first cake. Invert the second cake atop the frosting to form the second layer. Alternatively, the frosting may be transferred to a piping bag fitted with a nozzle of your choice and applied in this manner.

5. Frost the assembled cake with the remaining frosting.

1900s

To the average household, recipes of the 1900s were largely quaint, humble, and jovial echoes of decades past. Sweets and desserts were a high point to be enjoyed as a counterpoint to the revolving roster of bland dinner fare and the day's work of sweeping chimneys and being mauled by wayward horses.

For baking, the turn of the 20th century did not see many significant advancements, nor stark contrasts in methods or products. Flour mills had long since replaced their grindstones with metal rollers, allowing greater availability of higher-quality flour; baking powder had already been available for decades; and sugar was no longer off-limits to the home cook. What was new to this century of potential was the further rise of so-called "fireless cookery" and a greater dissemination of recipe books and bakers' knowledge taking advantage of the fact that replication of good baking was far easier when it wasn't done on an iron grate in your fireplace, or a coal-fired oven.

The recipes of the 1900s looked very little like those we find today, or indeed what you'll find in this book. They were tremendously undescriptive and took the form of just a list of ingredients, with unusual units of measurement like "butter the size of a walnut," "suitable amount of flour," or "a dessert spoon of lard." If there were instructions on mixing, they would be vague or abstruse, and seldom were there ever any clues on how long to bake, at what temperature, or even what to bake the item in. Things would begin to change toward the end of the decade, when an instructor at the Boston Cooking School, Ms. Fannie Merritt Farmer, had a vision that standardized measurements, detailed instructions, and an easily understood order of operations should be present in every recipe. While this idea soon began to take hold, it would take some time until this notion became ubiquitous.

The recipes in this section are a selection of forgotten mainstays, unusual delights, and down-to-earth echoes of the past. May they surprise you as they have surprised me, showing that our forefathers and -mothers had sweet tooths not unlike our own. Things were simply, and curiously, different.

Pecan Dainties

MACAROON • 1½ dozen

Prep: 25 minutes
Cook: 30 minutes

1½ cups (170g) pecan halves

White of 1 large egg

1 cup (220g) packed dark
   brown sugar

I'm wholly unsure of what dark, baker's magic our past generations involved themselves with, or what the potential repercussions of such are, but they were able to conjure something special from seemingly nothing. One look at this ingredient list might have you scratching your head, confused as to whether or not it'd actually amount to a baked good at all. Well, I can assure you it does. This classic dainty is a chewy, crunchy nugget of pecan goodness. If you're a fan of pecan pie, you're sure to love these little treats.

METHOD

1. Preheat the oven to 350°F (180°C).

2. Evenly spread the pecan halves on a baking sheet, and toast them for 10 minutes. Remove the nuts from the oven and let them cool. Reduce the oven temperature to 275°F (140°C).

3. In the bowl of a stand mixer fitted with a whisk attachment, or in a large bowl with which an electric hand mixer is to be used, beat the egg white to stiff peaks.

4. Gradually fold in the brown sugar. The mixture will deflate.

5. Roughly chop the cooled pecans and fold them into the mixture.

6. Drop by level tablespoon or small cookie scoop onto a parchment-lined baking sheet.

7. Bake at 275°F (140°C) for 17 to 18 minutes. The macaroons will still appear wet. Cool completely on the baking sheet and store in an airtight container.

Cornflake Macaroons

MACAROON · 2 dozen

Prep: 10 minutes
Cook: 20 minutes

Whites of 3 large eggs
½ tsp salt
1 tsp vanilla extract
1 cup (200g) granulated sugar
1 cup (120g) unsweetened
  shredded coconut
2 cups (65g) cornflake cereal

Cereal-flavored baked goods have come into vogue in the 21st century, attempting to capture childhood nostalgia for the meals that started many of our bygone days. Truth is, friends: it's old news. The inhabitants of the early 1900s were downright feral for the small, toasted flakes of corn invented by Dr. John Harvey Kellogg in 1894. So much so that they were put to use in everything from muffins to quick breads to pie crusts. In this recipe, they are paired perfectly with shredded coconut to create a crisp-shelled, chewy macaroon that is as unique as it is tasty.

METHOD

1. Preheat the oven to 350°F (180°C).

2. In the bowl of a stand mixer fitted with a whisk attachment, or in a large bowl with which an electric hand mixer is to be used, beat the egg whites and salt to stiff peaks. Beat in the vanilla.

3. Gradually fold in the sugar. The mixture will deflate.

4. Fold in the coconut and the cornflakes.

5. Drop by rounded tablespoon or cookie scoop onto a parchment-lined or greased baking sheet.

6. Bake for 18 to 22 minutes, or until macaroons take on a light golden color.

7. Cool completely on the baking sheet and store in an airtight container.

Food for the Gods

TORTE • 9-inch torte

Prep: 20 minutes
Cook: 40 minutes
Cool: 20 minutes

Whites of 3 large eggs

½ tsp salt

1 cup (200g) granulated sugar

½ cup (60g) fine graham
cracker crumbs

½ cup (75g) chopped, dried
apricot (any dried fruit may
be used: dates, figs,
currants)

½ cup (60g) chopped walnuts

This unorthodox dessert is sure to raise a few eyebrows and garner questions akin to: "what is it?" To which you might answer: "very good." Besides being good, classifying *Food for the Gods* is an unusual task as it bears very little resemblance to any modern dessert with which we are familiar, and the flamboyant name is hardly helpful. The dish supposedly acquired its name due to its use of expensive dried fruits and black walnuts. Many disparate modern desserts use this same name to indicate any and all that is good, and I choose to believe this century-old instance is no different. Notwithstanding, you might imagine this as a marshmallowy, fruited meringue with an amazing graham cracker nuttiness. My favorite way to make this is using dried apricots, though the call for "dried fruit" in early 1900s recipes would have certainly been answered with either dates or raisins. Served with some vanilla ice cream or whipped cream, it is a distinctive dessert winner.

METHOD

1. Preheat the oven to 325°F (165°C).

2. Line the bottom of a 9-inch (23-cm) springform pan or pie pan with a circle of parchment paper. Lightly grease both the parchment and sides of the pan.

3. In the bowl of a stand mixer fitted with a whisk attachment, or in a large bowl with which an electric hand mixer is to be used, beat the egg whites and salt to stiff peaks.

4. Gradually beat in the sugar, 2 tablespoons at a time, until stiff and glossy.

5. Gradually fold in the graham cracker crumbs, then fold in the dried fruit and walnuts.

6. Turn into the pan, smooth the top, and bake for 35 to 40 minutes. The top should be a pale gold color when done.

7. With the pan remaining in the oven, turn the oven off and leave the door ajar for 30 minutes to dry the meringue. After which, transfer to a wire rack and cool in the pan for 20 minutes.

8. Free the sides of the pan with a sharp knife and invert onto a serving dish or cutting board. Remove the parchment paper before serving.

TIP FROM YESTERYEAR
Use a springform pan if you have one, as it will allow the dessert to come out more easily, without breaking.

Cream Spice Cake

LAYER CAKE • Two 9-inch layers

Prep: 30 minutes
Cook: 40 minutes

CAKE

½ cup (115g) butter, softened

1 cup (220g) packed dark brown sugar

Yolks of 5 large eggs

2¼ (315g) cups all-purpose flour

2 tsp ground cinnamon

1 tsp ground cloves

1 tsp ground allspice

1 tsp ground mace (substitute with nutmeg)

¾ tsp salt

1 cup (250g) sour cream

½ tsp baking soda

FROSTING

1¾ cups (350g) granulated sugar

⅓ cup (80ml) light corn syrup, or golden syrup

½ cup (120ml) water

Whites of 2 large eggs

1 cup (115g) chopped walnuts

> **TIP FROM YESTERYEAR**
> Use the vanilla buttercream frosting recipe on page 25 for an easier frosting option.

Some nights I keep a mournful and sleepless vigil over my bedroom, shivering at the thought that today's breakneck experiments in cake-making will cast yesterday's unassuming, yet noble cakes beneath the blanket of forgotten history. I keep this vigil because I know an alarming number of us have yet to experience the good old spice cake, and thus yield to its charms. This *Cream Spice Cake* is a cake that does not dazzle you with pomp nor circumstance, but instead with assuredness in its identity and taste. The combination of spices is well-nigh curative, and paired with its traditional boiled frosting, this layer cake will be your most eager ally at any gathering.

CAKE METHOD

1. Preheat the oven to 325°F (165°C). Grease two 9-inch (23-cm) cake pans with butter and dust with flour.

2. Cream together the butter and brown sugar until light and fluffy. Beat in the egg yolks.

3. In another bowl, combine the flour, cinnamon, cloves, allspice, mace, and salt.

4. In a third bowl, mix together the sour cream and baking soda.

5. Working quickly, fold both the flour and sour cream mixtures into the creamed mixture, alternating the additions. Fold until barely combined.

6. Turn into the prepared pans and bake for 35 to 40 minutes, or until a toothpick inserted into the center can be removed cleanly.

7. Cool in the pans for 10 minutes before transferring to a wire rack to cool completely.

FROSTING METHOD

8. In a heavy-bottomed saucepan, boil the sugar, corn syrup, and water until the soft-ball stage is reached (240°F/115°C).

9. While the syrup is cooking, beat the egg whites to stiff peaks in a heatproof bowl with an electric hand mixer, or a stand mixer fitted with a whisk attachment.

10. With care, slowly pour the hot syrup down the side of the bowl with the egg whites while beating. Beat until the mixture cools and reaches a thick, spreadable consistency.

11. Spread a suitable amount of frosting evenly atop the first cake. Invert the second cake atop the first to form the second layer.

12. Frost the assembled cake with the remaining frosting. Decorate the top of the cake with coarsely chopped walnuts.

Sandtorte

CAKE • 9-inch springform

Prep: 20 minutes
Cook: 50 minutes
Cool: 1 hour

1 cup (225g) butter, softened

1 cup (200g) granulated sugar

Yolks of 6 large eggs, reserve whites

Grated zest of 1 lemon

3 tbsp black or gold rum

1 cup (128g) cornstarch

1 cup (140g) all-purpose flour

2 tsp baking powder

¼ tsp salt

Powdered sugar, for decorating

As a general rule, I'm quite inclined toward not having sand in my cakes. Sand in a cake is pretty high on my list of things that are both utterly unpleasant and completely avoidable, right beneath being trapped in a phone booth with a frenzied pigeon. However, this cake is only named so because its delicate crumb is as fine as sand. It is an ingenious, old-world, Germanic relative of the classic pound cake, based on the curious ratio of 1 part flour to 1 part cornstarch. To be a pound cake as we know it means to be rich, buttery, and regal. It also means being dense and hefty. This is not a bad thing by any stretch of the imagination, but imagine if that same rich flavor were to come with a feathery, melt-in-your-mouth lilt. Well heavens, you needn't imagine—this is a cookbook! And this is the *Sandtorte!* Let it introduce you to a texture and taste that is equal parts perplexing and delightful.

METHOD

1. Preheat your oven to 350°F (180°C). Grease a tall, 9-inch (23-cm) springform pan.

2. In the bowl of a stand mixer fitted with a paddle attachment, or in a large bowl with which an electric hand mixer is to be used, cream the butter and sugar until light and fluffy.

3. Begin adding the yolks of the 6 eggs (don't discard whites), beating very well after each addition. Add in the lemon zest and the rum.

4. While beating, add in the cornstarch two tablespoons at a time until the mixture is smooth. Then gradually beat in the flour, baking powder, and salt. Beat thoroughly for at least 5 minutes.

5. In a clean bowl, beat the egg whites to stiff peaks using a stand mixer or an electric hand mixer.

6. By hand, fold the egg whites into the batter in three additions. Fold until batter is silky smooth and there are no streaks remaining.

Turn into the prepared springform pan. Bake for 45 to 50 minutes, or until a toothpick inserted into the center can be removed with only a few small crumbs and the cake begins to pull away from the side. Cool in the pan for 10 minutes before transferring to a wire rack to cool completely, about 1 hour.

7. Once cooled, place a doily atop the cake and dust liberally with powdered sugar. Carefully remove the doily.

Election Cake
YEAST-RISEN CAKE • 10-inch Bundt

Prep: 3 hours 30 minutes
Cook: 45 minutes

SPONGE
2 packets active dry yeast (5¼ tsp/14g)

1½ cups (350ml) lukewarm water

1½ cups (210g) all-purpose flour

CAKE
1½ cups (240g) seedless raisins, golden raisins, or currants (or any combination of the three)

¼ cup (60ml) brandy

1¾ cup (245g) all-purpose flour

½ tsp salt

2 tsp ground cinnamon

1 tsp ground nutmeg

½ tsp ground cloves

½ tsp ground ginger

¾ cup (170g) butter, softened

1 cup (200g) granulated sugar

3 eggs, beaten

1 cup (115g) finely chopped pecans

GLAZE
2 tbsp whole milk

1 tbsp butter, softened

½ tsp vanilla extract

1 cup (120g) powdered sugar

A baker knows that yeast is used for breads, and baking powders and sodas are used for cakes. This cake says: incorrect. The history of the *Election Cake* is storied, and goes back well into the 18th century. Known then in colonial New England as muster cake, it was a treat to feed visitors traveling to towns where militia training was taking place. Later, it would become a celebratory symbol of American election days, which were then quite special occasions similar to any other holiday. This iteration pays homage to the age-old tradition, and takes the form of a sweet, fluffy, yeast-risen fruitcake imbued with the warm flavors of brandy and ginger. Paired with a simple glaze, you're likely to revel in its unusual pride.

SPONGE & CAKE METHOD
1. To create the sponge, sprinkle the yeast over the lukewarm water in a large bowl, before beating in the flour. Beat well until no lumps remain. Let stand in a warm place for 30 minutes while you continue. The sponge should bubble and increase in volume. Grease a 10-inch tube (25-cm) or Bundt pan with butter and dust with flour.

2. In a small bowl, soak the dried fruit in the brandy. In a separate bowl, sift together the flour, salt, cinnamon, nutmeg, cloves, and ginger.

3. In another large bowl, cream together the butter and sugar until light and fluffy. Gradually beat in the beaten eggs until smooth.

4. Add the sponge to the creamed mixture. Beat very well.

5. Gradually add in the flour and spice mixture, beating until smooth. Mix in the brandy, dried fruit, and chopped pecans.

6. Turn into the prepared pan, cover, and let rise in a warm place for 2 to 3 hours, or until the batter rises to roughly an inch below the pan's rim. Do not allow the batter to rise above the rim, lest it collapse in the oven.

7. Preheat your oven to 375°F (190°C).

8. Once risen, bake for 35 to 45 minutes, or until a toothpick inserted into the center can be removed cleanly. Let cool in the pan for 10 minutes before inverting onto a cooling rack to cool completely.

GLAZE METHOD
9. In a small saucepan over low heat, combine the milk and butter, stirring until the butter has melted.

10. Gradually whisk in the powdered sugar until smooth and slightly thickened. Remove from the heat and whisk in the vanilla. Pour over the cooled cake.

Pioneer Brownies

BAR • 9×13-inch pan

Prep: 15 minutes
Cook: 30 minutes

2 cups (400g) granulated sugar

½ cup (115g) butter, melted

2 large eggs

4oz (113g) unsweetened
chocolate, melted

2 tsp vanilla

1 cup (140g) all-purpose flour

1 cup (115g) chopped walnuts

Though the word "brownie" had been used previously to denote all manner of baked goods which were brown in color (these folks were very bright), the first recipe marrying "brownie" unto the chocolate cakey bar with which we are so familiar occurred in the early 1900s. For this, we have one Fannie Merritt Farmer to thank. Farmer was an American cooking instructor and pioneer of domestic science, nutrition, and level measurements during the late 19th and early 20th centuries, and much of the standardization of measurements and detailed instructions we find in today's cookbooks is certainly thanks to her. And, though I am forever indebted to Ms. Farmer for this, I am equally indebted to her for validating my belief that nuts do indeed belong in brownies. This recipe is arguably the first brownie (with crinkly skin included), and it's for those who are curious to taste the simple brilliance of that which started it all.

METHOD

1. Preheat the oven to 325°F (165°C).

2. Fashion a parchment paper sling within a 9×13-inch (23×33-cm) pan, greasing the exposed two sides of the pan.

3. Beat together the sugar and butter.

4. Using a whisk, add the eggs one at a time, beating smooth after each addition.

5. Whisk in the chocolate, followed by the vanilla.

6. Fold in the flour, and then fold in the walnuts.

7. Turn into the parchment-lined pan and bake for 25 to 30 minutes.

8. Allow the brownies to cool completely in the pan, then remove the brownies by grasping the sides of the parchment sling. Cut into bars.

Hot Cross Buns

YEAST BREAD • 1 dozen

Prep: 3 hours 30 minutes
Cook: 22 minutes

BUNS
¼ cup (55g) butter, softened

⅓ cup (75g) packed dark brown sugar

1 cup (235ml) whole milk

1½ cups (230g) raisins

2 packets active dry yeast (5¼ tsp/14g)

3½ cups (490g) bread flour, plus more if needed

1 tsp ground allspice

1 tbsp ground cinnamon

1 tsp salt

3 large eggs

CROSSES
½ cup (70g) all-purpose flour

Roughly 5 tbsp water

GLAZE
3 tbsp granulated sugar

3 tbsp water

In Bermuda, where I was born and raised, *Hot Cross Buns* are a staple of any Good Friday gathering worth its salt. We Bermudians slice one open and place a curried fish cake of salt cod between. Indeed, the same adoration is true in the United Kingdom during Easter time, minus the fish cake. However, *Hot Cross Buns* remain relatively unknown in the United States, and many there simply seem to think it's a nursery rhyme. How quaint. This spiced currant bun is the sweet, charismatic sister to the American dinner roll. It is a beautiful treat on its own, or with coffee, but stands out when it is sliced, toasted, and buttered.

BUNS METHOD

1. In a saucepan, combine the butter, brown sugar, milk, and raisins. Heat on low, stirring occasionally until the butter has melted and the sugar has dissolved. Remove from heat and let cool to lukewarm (below 100°F/38°C).

2. When the mixture is cool enough, stir in the yeast and let sit for 5 minutes to dissolve.

3. In the bowl of a stand mixer fitted with a dough hook, combine the bread flour, allspice, cinnamon, and salt.

4. Add the wet mixture into the dry ingredients, and begin kneading on medium speed.

5. Crack the eggs into a small bowl, and add one at a time to the dough with the stand mixer on. Let mix for 10 minutes.

6. After 10 minutes, turn off the stand mixer and let the dough rest for 15 minutes, before resuming mixing at a medium speed for another 5 minutes.

7. At this stage, if the dough presents impossibly wet, more flour may be added, 1 tablespoon at a time with the stand mixer on. More flour should only be added if the dough cannot be scraped from the bowl. This dough is inherently sticky.

8. Remove the dough from the bowl and place onto an unfloured countertop. Begin kneading.

9. After kneading for about 10 minutes, collect the dough and place it in a large, greased bowl. Cover and let rise in a warm place for about 1½ to 2 hours.

10. Preheat your oven to 375°F (190°C).

11. Remove the dough from the bowl, and divide into 12 equal pieces. To roll into balls, place dough onto an unfloured surface, and roll in circular motions with a cupped hand. This should result in a uniform, smooth ball.

continues...

12. Place balls at equal distances in a parchment-lined 9×13-inch (23×33-cm) baking pan that has had its sides greased. Let proof for roughly 1 hour.

CROSSES METHOD

13. If adding crosses, mix together the ½ cup of all-purpose flour and 5 tablespoons water to form a paste. Add paste to a piping bag, and pipe thin lines down the proofed dough to form crosses.

14. Bake for roughly 20 to 22 minutes, or until the tops of the buns are a light golden brown.

GLAZE METHOD

15. While the buns are baking, combine the 3 tablespoons water and 3 tablespoons sugar for the glaze in a small saucepan. Bring to a light simmer.

16. As soon as the buns are out of the oven, brush the tops with the sugar mixture. Cool completely before storing in an airtight container.

TIP FROM YESTERYEAR

This hot cross bun dough is very enriched, meaning it contains added fat and sugar to make for a luxurious spiced bun. However, this also means that it will initially seem nearly impossible to knead on your counter. It will want to stick to everything. Accept this fate. The use of a bench scraper makes this fight possible.

With the dough on the counter, begin pulling the edges out, and then folding back over into the center of the dough. Continue this process on opposing edges. Use your bench scraper to collect that which sticks to the counter, occasionally gathering all the dough and inverting back upon the counter to ensure new angles are being kneaded. The more you knead, the more manageable the dough becomes and the less it sticks.

Hermits

COOKIE • 4 dozen

Prep: 20 minutes
Cook: 12 minutes

½ cup lard (100g) or butter (115g), softened

1 cup (200g) granulated sugar

2 large eggs

2 cups (280g) all-purpose flour

1 tsp ground cinnamon

1 tsp ground nutmeg

½ tsp ground cloves

½ tsp salt

½ tsp baking soda

½ cup (120ml) buttermilk

1 cup (160g) raisins

½ cup (75g) chopped dates

½ cup (60g) chopped walnuts

One might be drawn to *Hermits* due to the perplexing name and the sheer quantity of recipes bearing the title in prewar cookbooks. For a time they were seemingly inevitable and inescapable—the chocolate chip cookie of old, if you will. I describe these cookies as tasting like a hug from a humble and portly old lady wearing a wool cardigan. Unpretentious, warming, and lovingly spiced; they stand as one of the exemplary OG cookies. At its core, a hermit denotes a chewy cookie containing dried fruit and nuts, spiced with cinnamon, cloves, and nutmeg.

METHOD

1. Preheat the oven to 375°F (190°C).

2. In a large bowl, cream together the lard and sugar until light and fluffy. Beat in the eggs one at a time.

3. In a separate bowl, combine the flour, cinnamon, nutmeg, cloves, salt, and baking soda. Add to the creamed mixture alternately with the buttermilk.

4. Fold in the raisins, dates, and walnuts.

5. Drop by rounded tablespoon or cookie scoop onto a parchment-lined baking sheet.

6. Bake for 10 to 12 minutes. Briefly cool on the sheet, then transfer to a wire rack to cool completely.

1910s

The 1910s were a time of product variety, growing grocery chains, packaged baked goods, and an incremental step toward more easily replicable home baked goods through readily available tomes of knowledge. Everyone from baking powder manufacturers, flour mills, chocolatiers, and vegetable shortening companies had their own cookbooks detailing the swaths of recipes that could be made utilizing their products. Also, cars had to be started by cranking a large lever on the front of the automobile, an interesting feature which often literally broke the arms of many unsuspecting motorists, but this is unrelated.

The previously mentioned Fannie Merritt Farmer had bombshell cookbooks released, including *A New Book of Cookery: Eight-Hundred and Sixty Recipes Covering the Whole Range of Cookery* in 1912, and *The Priscilla Cook Book for Everyday Housekeepers* in 1913. These cookbooks helped make the art of a good, easy-to-follow recipe a thing of want and praise.

Through newspaper columns and the growth of low-volume community cookbooks, homegrown ideas also began to reach other curious bakers, giving birth to a burgeoning realm of pedestrian recipes. This would help cement some of the now-famed regional peculiarities for years to come, and allow unique takes, interesting perspectives, and previously guarded family recipes to enter countless kitchens.

This section plays host to both ritzy classics and homegrown curios, and although the 1910s may still feel far removed from today's kitchens, I think you will be pleasantly surprised with how beautifully this decade's creations will grace your table.

Starchies

COOKIE • 2 dozen

Prep: 10 minutes
Cook: 20 minutes

½ cup (120ml) sweetened condensed milk

½ cup (115g) butter, softened

2 cups (256g) cornstarch

Three simple ingredients have absolutely no right to make some of the cutest, tastiest morsels of baking. Yet they do, and I'm almost mad about it. Crumbly, soft, and delicate, the country of Brazil is to thank for the creation of these cookies in the early 20th century, where they are known as Sequilhos, or Biscoitos de Maizena. If you're ever in want of a unique, simple, and utterly photogenic cookie (that happens to be gluten-free!) for your coffee spread or teatime treat, *Starchies* are your answer.

METHOD

1. Preheat the oven to 325°F (165°C).

2. In a large bowl, combine the sweetened condensed milk and the butter. Beat smooth.

3. Using the handle of a wooden spoon, stir in the cornstarch two tablespoons at a time. Mix until a smooth dough is formed.

4. Divide by rounded teaspoon or small cookie scoop, lightly rolling in the hands to form a smooth 2-inch (5-cm) ball. Place on a parchment-lined baking sheet.

5. Bake for 15 to 20 minutes. Cookies should not brown. Let cool briefly on the baking sheet before transferring to a wire rack to cool completely.

Pork Cake

QUICKBREAD • 9×5-inch loaf

Prep: 20 minutes
Cook: 1 hour 30 minutes

½ lb (225g) ground pork

⅔ cup (160ml) water

1 cup (200g) granulated sugar

1 tsp ground cinnamon

1 tsp ground nutmeg

1 tsp ground cloves

1 tsp baking soda

½ tsp salt

2 large eggs

⅓ cup (80ml) molasses

1⅓ cup (213g) raisins

1⅓ cup (200g) chopped dates

2 cups (280g) all-purpose flour,
plus more if needed

Yes, there is ground pork in this cake, and yes, the initial reactions to this realization are often confused and filled with a few choice expletives. The absurdity of this recipe is what led it to become the first one I ever baked on TikTok in 2020, and what resulted was nothing short of absolute surprise. I have since baked this cake with comedian Jay Leno, actress and comedian Ayo Edebiri, and entertainer Kelly Clarkson; and for what it's worth, Clarkson liked it. Pork is a very fatty meat, and its use in baking in place of lard or butter during times where those ingredients might've been difficult to come by was not uncommon. It offers moisture, a rich texture, and good conversation. The *Pork Cake* is a true, dark fruitcake, worthy of any Christmastime feast. You don't taste the pork so much as you gently—perhaps warily—feel its presence. It's a sweet richness unlike anything else. If you're interested in baking a traditional fruitcake with a historical, wacky twist, look no further.

METHOD

1. Preheat the oven to 350°F (180°C). Grease a 9×5-inch (23×13-cm) loaf pan.

2. In a large saucepan or skillet, combine the ground pork and water. Bring to a boil and let boil for 2 minutes. Remove from heat to cool. Do not discard water.

3. In a large bowl, combine the sugar, cinnamon, nutmeg, cloves, baking soda, salt, eggs, molasses, raisins, and dates.

4. Add in the ground pork and its water, beating vigorously for 2 to 3 minutes.

5. Gradually beat in the flour to make a stiff, barely pourable batter. Another ½ cup (70g) of flour may be added if the batter is too thin. This will vary on account of the nature of the ground pork used.

6. Turn into the prepared pan and bake for 70 to 90 minutes, or until a toothpick inserted into the center can be removed cleanly.

7. Cool in the pan for 10 minutes before transferring to a wire rack to cool completely before slicing.

Admiral's Gingerbread

QUICKBREAD • 9×5-inch loaf

Prep: 30 minutes
Cook: 55 minutes

1 cup (225g) butter, softened
1½ cups (210g) all-purpose flour
2 tbsp ground ginger
3 tbsp molasses or treacle
Yolks of 5 large eggs, reserve whites
½ tsp salt
1½ cups (180g) powdered sugar
1 tsp baking powder

I love gingerbread almost as much as I love hot takes and novel perspectives on classic bakes, and the *Admiral's Gingerbread* has both. This is a most peculiar variety of gingerbread, and its bizarre method of preparation seems to have been quite popular along the East Coast cities of the United States in the early 1910s under names like New York Gingerbread and Providence Gingerbread. Bakers will notice that it has an impressively ass-backwards order of operation, but despite this (or because of it), the result is a surprisingly soft, light, and buttery ginger loaf, setting itself apart from the traditional dense, dark gingerbreads of yuletide. It is a simple and happy pairing with morning coffee or afternoon tea.

METHOD

1. Preheat the oven to 350°F (180°C). Grease a 9×5-inch (23×13-cm) loaf pan.

2. In a large bowl, beat the butter until smooth and light. Gradually beat in the flour, ginger, and molasses. Beat until smooth.

3. In a separate bowl, whisk together the egg yolks and the salt. Gradually whisk in the powdered sugar.

4. In the bowl of a stand mixer fitted with a whisk attachment, or in a large bowl with which an electric hand mixer is to be used, beat the reserved egg whites to stiff peaks. Beat in the baking powder.

5. Mix the egg yolk mixture into the creamed mixture, before adding the egg white mixture. Beat thoroughly.

6. Turn into the prepared pan and bake for 50 to 55 minutes, or until a toothpick inserted into the center can be removed cleanly.

7. Cool in the pan for 10 minutes before transferring to a wire rack to cool completely before slicing.

Chocolate Potato Cake

CAKE • 8×8-inch cake

Prep: 45 minutes
Cook: 50 minutes

CAKE

½ medium russet potato
½ cup (120ml) whole milk
½ cup (115g) butter, softened
1 cup (200g) granulated sugar
2 large eggs, beaten
1 cup (140g) all-purpose flour
2 tsp baking powder
½ tsp ground cinnamon
½ tsp ground cloves
½ tsp ground nutmeg
2oz (60g) semisweet chocolate, grated
½ cup (60g) chopped walnuts

ICING

2 tbsp butter, softened
1 cup (200g) granulated sugar
½ cup (60ml) whole milk
2oz (60g) semisweet chocolate
½ tsp vanilla extract

History holds many baking secrets, and among those secrets are clever ways to achieve a perfect cake texture. Where modern methods will have you scientifically measuring cake flour down to the nanogram, taking the temperature of eggs as if they have the flu, or speaking in hushed tones so as to not disturb a baking cake— the bakers of yesteryear simply said: "throw a potato in there!" And they were right. The *Chocolate Potato Cake* is my favorite recipe I've had the pleasure to explore. It is humble, moist, and perfectly captures the vintage flavors of years past, while nodding to the inner chocolate-lover of today. Its secrets not only lie with the moisture-holding starches of the potato, but also with the grated chocolate that doesn't quite melt completely during baking. It is a chocolate cake unlike any other.

CAKE METHOD

1. Preheat the oven to 350°F (180°C). Grease an 8×8-inch (20×20-cm) cake pan with butter and dust with flour.

2. In a small saucepan, bring water to a boil. Wash and dice the potato. Do not peel. Add the potato to the water and boil until fork tender. Drain, then mash in a small bowl (you should end up with about ¾ cup mashed potato) before stirring in the milk.

3. In a large bowl, cream together the butter and sugar until light and fluffy. Beat in the beaten eggs.

4. Add the milk and potato mixture to the creamed mixture, beating well.

5. In a separate bowl, mix the flour, baking powder, cinnamon, cloves, and nutmeg before folding this into the wet ingredients.

6. Mix in the grated chocolate and the chopped walnuts

7. Turn into the prepared pan and bake for 45 to 50 minutes, or until a toothpick inserted into the center can be removed cleanly.

8. Cool in the pan for 10 minutes before transferring to a wire rack to cool completely.

ICING METHOD

9. In a saucepan over medium heat, combine the butter, sugar, milk, and chocolate. Bring to a boil, then reduce heat to a gentle simmer for 8 minutes, stirring occasionally. Remove from heat.

10. Add the vanilla and beat the frosting with a whisk or an electric hand mixer until cooled and thickened. Spread or pour over the cooled cake.

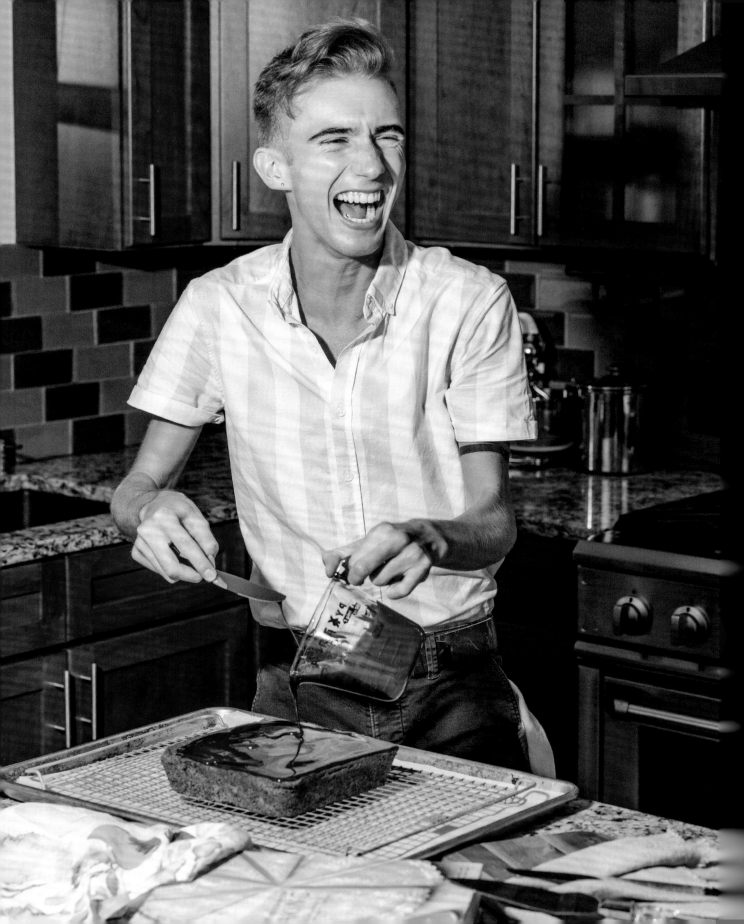

The Lady Baltimore

LAYER CAKE • Two 9-inch layers

Prep: 30 minutes
Cook: 35 minutes

CAKE
½ cup (115g) butter, softened
1½ cup (300g) granulated sugar
2¼ cup (315g) all-purpose flour
2 tsp baking powder
1 tsp salt
1 cup (235ml) whole milk
Whites of 4 large eggs
1 tbsp lemon juice

FILLING
¾ cup (110g) finely chopped candied cherries, or drained, dried, and chopped maraschino cherries
¾ cup (120g) finely chopped dried figs
½ cup (80g) finely chopped raisins
½ cup (60g) finely chopped walnuts
Roughly ¼ cup (60ml) prepared frosting (below)

BOILED FROSTING
2 cups (400g) granulated sugar
⅓ cup (80ml) light corn syrup, or golden syrup
⅓ cup (80ml) water
Whites of 2 large eggs
1 tsp vanilla extract

The Lady Baltimore is a cake of legend, renown, and utter sophistication. She is also humble and unpretentious. Just how she manages to be both is a question to which I've yet to find an answer. The delightful fruit and nut filling, delicate white layers, and classic boiled frosting help to secure her as one of the most famed early 20th century cakes. Just as now-dead people enjoyed *The Lady Baltimore* when she first began to grace tables, your resurrection of her will be a moment to savor.

CAKE METHOD

1. Preheat the oven to 350°F (180°C). Grease two 9-inch (23-cm) cake pans with butter and dust with flour.

2. In a large bowl, cream together the butter and sugar until light and fluffy.

3. In a separate bowl, combine the flour, baking powder, and salt. Add to the creamed mixture alternately with the milk.

4. In the bowl of a stand mixer fitted with a whisk attachment, or in a large bowl with which an electric hand mixer is to be used, beat the egg whites and lemon juice to stiff peaks. Fold into the batter in 3 additions.

5. Turn the batter into the prepared pans and bake for 30 to 35 minutes, or until a toothpick inserted into the center can be removed cleanly and the cake pulls away from the sides of the pan.

6. Cool in the pans for 10 minutes before transferring to a wire rack to cool completely.

FILLING & BOILED FROSTING METHOD

7. In a large bowl, combine the filling ingredients, save for the prepared frosting.

8. In a heavy-bottomed saucepan, boil the sugar, corn syrup, and water until the soft-ball stage is reached (240°F/115°C).

9. While the syrup is cooking, beat the egg whites to stiff peaks in a heatproof bowl with an electric hand mixer, or a stand mixer fitted with a whisk attachment.

10. With care, slowly pour the hot syrup down the side of the bowl with the egg whites while beating. Beat until the mixture cools and reaches a thick, spreadable consistency. About 4 to 5 minutes. Finally, add the vanilla.

11. Working quickly, blend roughly ¼ cup (60ml) prepared frosting to the filling ingredients. More frosting may be required for a uniform filling.

12. Spread the filling evenly atop the first cake. Invert the second cake atop the filling to form the second layer. Frost the assembled cake with the remaining frosting. Decorate the top of the cake with walnuts and candied cherries.

ANZAC Biscuits

COOKIE • 2½ dozen

Prep: 20 minutes
Cook: 10 minutes

---

1 cup (90g) rolled oats

1¼ cup (175g) all-purpose flour

1 cup (120g) unsweetened, shredded coconut

¾ cup (150g) granulated sugar

¼ tsp salt

⅔ cup (150g) butter, softened

¼ cup (60ml) golden syrup

1 tsp baking soda

My absolute favorite variety of oatmeal cookie. But be wary, don't ever call *ANZAC Biscuits* cookies—you'll be shot. They are definitely a biscuit, as any Aussie or New Zealander will tell you. Appearing in Australian and New Zealand newspapers and cookbooks before the turn of the 1920s, these biscuits became a feature of these nations' home fronts during World War I. They have long since been associated with the *A*ustralian and *N*ew *Z*ealand *A*rmy *C*orps. Legend has it that they were famed for their ability to keep well and safe when shipped from home shores to soldiers abroad, however I prefer to praise them further for their delectable taste and unrivaled texture. Utterly buttery and crispy on the outside, and chewy in their centers, this biscuit's flavors of coconut and oats are just plain tasty and wholesome.

METHOD

1. Preheat the oven to 350°F (180°C).

2. In a large bowl, combine the oats, flour, coconut, sugar, and salt. Set aside.

3. In a saucepan over medium heat, combine the butter and golden syrup until the butter has melted.

4. Remove from heat and add the baking soda, stirring briefly. The mixture should begin to fizz.

5. Immediately add the saucepan ingredients to the dry ingredients and mix quickly until barely combined.

6. Drop by tablespoon or small cookie scoop onto a parchment-lined or greased baking sheet and bake for 9 to 11 minutes. Cool briefly on the baking sheet before transferring to a wire rack to cool completely.

TIP FROM YESTERYEAR
Golden syrup is a type of treacle popular in British realms. It can be approximately substituted by mixing three parts light corn syrup with one part molasses. For this recipe, use 3 tablespoons of light corn syrup with 1 tablespoon of molasses.

Rice Pudding

BAKED DESSERT • 6 servings

Prep: 25 minutes
Cook: 1 hour 20 minutes

½ cup (100g) uncooked white
rice (not long grain)

1 cup (235ml) water

¼ tsp salt

2 cups (470ml) whole milk

Yolks of 3 large eggs, beaten

½ cup (100g) granulated sugar

½ cup (80g) seedless raisins

¼ tsp ground nutmeg

1 tsp ground cinnamon

To the uninitiated, the use of rice in a dessert may seem unusual. However, this classic pud is of a variety that has been enjoyed across the globe for thousands of years. Once an elite and expensive meal of British royalty—later becoming a pedestrian dessert of the commoners when imported rice became ubiquitous—*Rice Pudding* means many things to many people. This recipe captures the modest appeal of a warm, spiced pudding, and is guaranteed to stick to your ribs and fill you with the gentle glow of the past

METHOD

1. Preheat the oven to 350°F (180°C). Grease a 1 ½- or 2-quart (1.4 or 1.9L) casserole dish.

2. In a small pot over medium heat, combine the rice, water, and salt. Once boiling, cook for 15 to 18 minutes until rice is tender. Drain any excess liquid, and transfer to a heatproof bowl.

3. Mix in the remaining ingredients until well combined.

4. Pour into the prepared dish, and place the casserole dish into a larger roasting pan, filling the roasting pan with enough boiling water to reach at least halfway up the casserole dish. It is best to add the water once the pans are in the oven, to reduce the risk of spilling hot water.

5. Bake for 50 to 60 minutes, or until the pudding is set. Serve warm.

Carrot Pie

PIE • 9-inch pie

Prep: 45 minutes
Cook: 1 hour

1 single-crust pie pastry
(page 24)

1½ lbs (700g) of carrots, peeled
and chopped

½ cup (120ml) heavy cream

3 tbsp butter, melted

1 cup (220g) packed dark
brown sugar

2 large eggs

1 tsp salt

2 tsp ground cinnamon

1 tsp ground nutmeg

½ tsp ground ginger

¼ tsp ground cloves

2 tbsp all-purpose flour

You've had your fair share of pumpkin pie. You're over the repetition, you're wanting to spice things up and be a little quirky. The folks of the 1910s had the answer when they seemingly ran out of pumpkins, and in a manic stupor clawed for the nearest similarly-colored vegetable. But they created no substitution, they created a veritable masterpiece. The *Carrot Pie* combines the joys of autumn spices with the sweet nuttiness of the carrot, and the result is far more than the sum of its parts. Enjoy it at your own risk, for you may never look at a pumpkin pie the same.

METHOD

1. Preheat the oven to 400°F (205°C).

2. Fit your prepared bottom pie crust in a standard 9-inch (23-cm) pan (not a deep pie pan); line with parchment paper; and fill with pie weights or dry beans. Par-bake for 12 to 15 minutes, or until the pastry begins to color. Place the pan on a wire rack to cool, remove the parchment paper and pie weights.

3. Place the chopped carrots in a large saucepan or pot and fill with enough water to cover. Simmer until the carrots are fork tender, roughly 30 minutes.

4. Thoroughly drain off the water and return carrots to the heat to remove any excess moisture, roughly 5 minutes. Transfer to a large bowl and cool slightly.

5. Thoroughly mash the carrots with a potato masher or a ricer, ensuring the mixture is as smooth as possible. This process can be finished with a fork for a finer mash. Alternatively, this can be done in a food processor, or the cooled carrots can be added to a blender with the heavy cream and pureed smooth.

6. Thoroughly mix remaining ingredients into the carrot mixture and pour into the par-baked pie crust. Lower the oven temperature to 350°F (180°C). Bake for 50 to 60 minutes. The center should be nearly set, but still a bit wobbly.

7. Allow the pie to cool to room temperature before serving. Pie may also be covered and refrigerated after it has reached room temperature, and served cold.

Divinity

CONFECTION • 1 dozen

**Prep: 30 minutes
Cool: Overnight**

2 cups (400g) granulated sugar

½ cup (120ml) corn syrup

½ cup (120ml) water

Whites of 2 large eggs

1 tsp vanilla extract

1 cup (115g) chopped pecans, or any chopped nut

½ cup (80g) chopped candied cherries, or any dried/ candied fruit (optional)

Divinity is a peculiar concern: part nougat, part marshmallow, part meringue. A soft and delectable chew gives way to jovial encounters of fruit and crunchy nuts, all amidst the sweet embrace of vanilla. There is nothing else in its class, and although our modern notion of candy is far removed from that of the 1910s, I can still easily concur with this recipe's naming convention: It is rather divine.

METHOD

1. Combine the sugar, corn syrup, and water in a heavy-bottomed saucepan.

2. Over high heat, boil the syrup until it reaches the hard-ball stage (260°F/127°C). While the syrup boils, beat the egg whites to stiff peaks in a heatproof bowl using an electric hand mixer or stand mixer.

3. As soon as the syrup mixture reaches 260°F (127°C), remove from heat and slowly pour the syrup in a thin stream down the side of the bowl of egg whites while beating.

4. Continue to beat until the mixture thickens and holds its shape firmly. This should take 8 to 10 minutes.

5. Quickly beat in the vanilla, and then mix in the nuts and fruit.

6. Drop by heaping tablespoons onto wax paper. Alternatively, pour into a 9×9-inch (23×23-cm) parchment-lined and lightly greased pan to be later cut into squares.

7. Let dry uncovered at room temperature for at least 12 hours, or overnight.

TIP FROM YESTERYEAR
Divinity prepared in a pan should be left to dry at room temperature for a full 24 hours before being cut, whereas those dropped onto parchment can be successfully dried in 12.

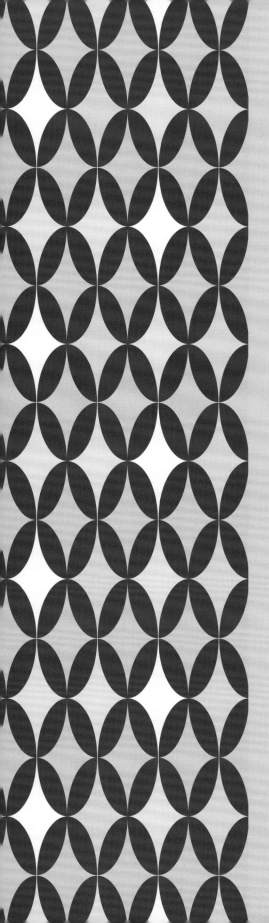

1920s

As a jazz pianist, I'm positively enthralled with the 1920s. Besides the obvious Prohibition, the decade was colored by the flourishing of jazz, art deco styling, lengthening cars, and a sense of America coming into its own. Despite the images of opulent parties, shining silverware, and towering plates of canapés and dessert spreads, the average home baker's kitchen was not so gilded, and nor were their creations. But that didn't mean that a greater variety of recipes didn't find themselves in front of the family.

Before the 1920s, bread was arguably the foremost baked good from the oven. It was an important, nutritive, and basic staple of the table. But, with falling sugar and produce prices, paired with higher grade flour becoming available, the housewives of the roaring twenties found softer cakes and fruity desserts increasingly within reach, and the simple bread no longer needed to take precedence.

Through growing avenues of printing and publishing, the 1920s also saw a greater sharing of recipes between disparate parts of the nation. Those in Vermont could faithfully reproduce the latest Georgia cornbread, and New York gingerbread found its way onto tables in Florida. Baking was steadily becoming more of a growing home pastime, and not just a necessary activity to produce plain bread. That was, until the stock market crash plunged the world into the Great Depression in 1929. Whoops!

The decade's bakes included in this section showcase the results of expanding tastes and recipe varieties, and it also includes a brief glimpse at the response during the very start of the Depression.

Ricciarelli

MACAROON • 1½ dozen

Prep: 1 hour 30 minutes
Cook: 25 minutes

2 cups (210g) almond flour

1½ cups (180g) powdered
   sugar, divided

¼ tsp baking powder

Whites of 2 large eggs

¾ tsp salt

1 tsp lemon juice

Zest of 1 lemon

2 tsp vanilla extract

2 tsp almond extract

I believe that the modern western cookie has fallen victim to the malady of sameness. Though they may vary with their add-ins: chocolate chips, nuts, and other accoutrements, they end up being the same round disk in different clothes. I found an antidote to this condition when I embraced the macaroon and similar cookies that strayed from the butter, eggs, and leavened flour foundation. *Ricciarelli* are a Tuscan almond macaroon that had been enjoyed centuries before the 1920s. However, its export beyond the bounds of Italy and the experiments that followed in foreign cookbooks gave way to *Ricciarelli* of citrus, vanilla, and even maple flavors. I find this variety to be my favorite: soft; almondy; and full of bright, zesty lemon. All dusted under a crinkled blanket of powdered sugar. I have yet to find a cookie better suited to a late morning coffee, and I have full faith you will agree.

METHOD

1. In a medium bowl, sift together the almond flour, 1 cup (120g) powdered sugar, and baking powder.

2. In the bowl of a stand mixer fitted with a whisk attachment, or in a large bowl with which an electric hand mixer is to be used, beat the egg whites, salt, and lemon juice to stiff peaks. Fold in the lemon zest.

3. In small additions, sift the dry ingredients directly into the egg white and lemon mixture, folding thoroughly after each addition. Deflation of the egg whites is to be expected. Add the vanilla and almond extract midway through this process.

4. Pinch off 1½ tbsp of dough (#60 cookie scoop) and roll in the hand to form balls. Roll thoroughly in the remaining ½ cup (60g) of powdered sugar and place on a parchment-lined baking sheet.

5. Leave the formed dough to dry on the baking sheet for an hour, before lightly flattening each ball with two fingers. A cookie stamp, or a glass with a decorative indentation may also be used.

6. Preheat the oven to 325°F (165°C).

7. Bake for 20 to 25 minutes.

8. Cool briefly on the baking sheet before carefully transferring to a wire rack to cool completely.

Hedgehogs

COOKIE • 4 dozen

Prep: 1 hour 20 minutes
Cook: 15 minutes

---

2 cups (230g) chopped walnuts

1 cup (150g) chopped dates

2 cups (170g) unsweetened desiccated coconut, divided

1 cup (220g) packed dark brown sugar

2 large eggs, divided

Hedgehogs are cute, and for that reason most of us are averse to eating them. They also have spines, and this poses a logistical issue. The bakers of yesteryear resolved instead to adorably approximate these mammals using dates, walnuts, and coconut. It just so happens that they are as tasty as they are endearing, and their chewy, brown-sugary goodness, coated in a lovable layer of coconut, tops off an ingenious way to create a unique cookie.

METHOD

1. If one possesses a food processor, the walnuts, dates, 1 cup (85g) of coconut, brown sugar, and 1 egg may be added and processed to a fine paste (about 3 to 5 minutes). Proceed to step 4.

2. Without a food processor, mince the walnuts and dates to a fine paste using a food chopper or blender.

3. Transfer to a large bowl, and thoroughly mix in 1 cup (85g) coconut, brown sugar, and 1 egg.

4. Divide the dough in fourths, and using wet hands, roll into 1-inch diameter ropes. This should make four 15-inch (38-cm) long ropes of even girth. Cover and chill in the fridge for at least 1 hour.

5. Preheat the oven to 350°F (180°C).

6. In a small bowl, beat the remaining egg.

7. Cut each rope into 12 pieces of equal length by first dividing each rope into thirds, and then halving each third twice.

8. Dip pieces in the beaten egg before rolling them in the remaining 1 cup (85g) of coconut. Place at equal distances on a parchment-lined baking sheet.

9. Bake for 15 minutes. As these do not spread, all four dozen may be baked at once on a full-size sheet. Cool completely on the baking sheet before serving.

TIP FROM YESTERYEAR
This recipe calls for desiccated coconut, which is a very finely ground, unsweetened, dried coconut product. Unsweetened shredded coconut can work in its place, but it is important to use the finest textured and driest variety you can find.

Maple-Squash Gems

MUFFIN • 1 dozen

Prep: 30 minutes
Cook: 33 minutes

---

1 cup (250g) peeled butternut
    squash

½ cup (120ml) water, reserved
    from drained squash

2 tbsp butter, melted

½ cup (120ml) maple syrup

2 cups (280g) all-purpose flour

¼ tsp salt

1 tsp ground cinnamon

3 tsp baking powder

2 large eggs, well beaten

1 cup (160g) golden raisins,
    if desired

There are good, simple gems, and then there are good, simple gems with ingenious quirks. This recipe is in the latter category. Now, you might be wondering what a gem is: It is dead-people talk for a muffin. Specifically, the little cast-iron pans forged with ornate patterns in which muffins, biscuits, and small cakes were baked. Should you happen to have a vintage cast-iron gem pan, you could be really authentic with these boys! But no matter what you bake them in, you'll hear a century-old whisper of what the yuppified pumpkin spice craze was to become: A gay muffin with a subtle winning trio of maple, cinnamon, and nutty squash flavors. The squash keeps these delectably moist and makes them most welcome on your breakfast plate. Serve them with salted butter or any manner of marmalade.

METHOD

1. Preheat the oven to 350°F (180°C). Grease a standard muffin pan (muffins will stick to paper liners).

2. Cut enough peeled squash to equal 1 cup when mashed (the uncooked weight will roughly reflect the boiled weight). Transfer to a small pot and cover with water. Boil on high heat until fork-tender, about 15 minutes.

3. When draining the squash, reserve ½ cup (120ml) of the squash water before draining completely.

4. Mash the squash in the pot with a potato masher or a fork. Measure out 1 cup (250g) and transfer to a heatproof bowl.

5. Add the squash water, melted butter, and maple syrup, and cool to lukewarm.

6. Meanwhile, combine the flour, salt, cinnamon, and baking powder in a separate bowl.

7. Once the squash mixture is lukewarm, mix in the well beaten eggs.

8. Add the dry ingredients and mix until no dry flour remains. Do not overmix.

9. Fold in the golden raisins, if using.

10. Fill the prepared muffin pan cups three-quarters full, and bake for 28 to 33 minutes, or until a toothpick inserted into the center can be removed cleanly.

11. Cool briefly in the pan before turning them out onto a wire rack to cool completely.

Poorman's Pie

PIE • 9-inch pie

Prep: 30 minutes
Cook: 25 minutes
Cool: 2 hours

1 single-crust pie pastry
   (page 24)
¼ cup (35g) all-purpose flour
2 cups (470ml) whole milk
1½ cups (300g) granulated
   sugar
2 tsp vanilla extract
Nutmeg, for garnish

Milk and sugar a pie does not make. Not unless you know how to tame those two ingredients, and that is something our Great Depression pioneers knew how to do at the start of the financial crisis. Without tasting this fantastic custard pie, it's difficult to attempt to convince you that it is so much more than the sum of its meager ingredients. Perhaps this is one point in favor of magic. The history of this pie is tangled, to say the least, with not too dissimilar recipes emerging from the Amish, Shaker, and Quaker communities long before the Great Depression hit. What is certain is that this simple method became a widespread success during the Depression, and not entirely because of its frugal nature: it also tastes really good. So good, in fact, that successors to this version became the unofficial state pie of Indiana in 2009, where it is known as Sugar Cream Pie, or Hoosier Pie.

METHOD

1. Preheat the oven to 425°F (220°C).

2. Fit your prepared bottom pie crust in a standard 9-inch (23-cm) pan (not a deep pie pan); line with parchment paper; and fill with pie weights or dry beans. Par-bake for 15 minutes, or until the pastry begins to color. Place the pan on a wire rack to cool, remove the parchment paper and pie weights.

3. Reduce oven temperature to 375°F (190°C) before preparing the filling.

4. In a large saucepan over medium-high heat, add the flour and slowly begin whisking in the milk to avoid clumping. Whisk in the granulated sugar.

5. Bring the mixture to a boil, and boil for about 3 minutes. Remove from the heat and stir in the vanilla.

6. Pour into the par-baked pie shell, and evenly sprinkle nutmeg atop. Bake for 20 to 25 minutes, or until the custard is set.

7. Let the pie cool to room temperature and solidify on a wire rack for 2 hours before serving. Pie may be refrigerated after this point and served cold.

Dutch Apple Cake

UPSIDE-DOWN CAKE • 9-inch cake

Prep: 30 minutes
Cook: 35 minutes

BOTTOM LAYER
2 tbsp butter, softened
½ cup (110g) packed dark brown sugar
¼ tsp grated nutmeg
2 cups (215g) thinly sliced apples (Granny Smith, Gala, or Honeycrisp)

CAKE
2 cups (280g) all-purpose flour
1 tsp baking soda
1 tsp salt
½ cup (100g) granulated sugar
¼ tsp ground mace (substitute with nutmeg)
½ tsp ground cinnamon
½ cup (115g) butter, cold
¾ cup (180ml) buttermilk
1 large egg

When many think of old-timey baking, the pineapple upside down cake invariably comes to mind. So much so that other varieties of upside-down cake are forgotten and left on read. This is worth mourning, as this classic *Dutch Apple Cake* waits patiently to share its warm, caramelized apples set atop a fluffy spiced crumb with you, and you should feel very bad about denying it the opportunity. Oft-associated with the Pennsylvania Dutch who have long settled on the East Coast of the United States and are well-known for their apple cakes and pies, this recipe harkens to the broader adoration of fruit-topped "breakfast cakes" during the mid-1920s. When care is taken to arrange the apple layer in a delightful pattern, those seated at your table will sing its praises long before it even reaches their mouths.

BOTTOM LAYER METHOD

1. Preheat the oven to 375°F (190°C).

2. Liberally rub a 9-inch (23-cm) cake pan with the softened butter. Combine the brown sugar and nutmeg, and sprinkle into the pan. Decoratively arrange the sliced apples over this sugar mixture.

CAKE METHOD

3. In a large bowl, combine the flour, baking soda, salt, sugar, mace, and cinnamon. Cut the cold butter into small cubes.

4. Using a pastry cutter or a fork, mash the butter into the dry ingredients until a crumbly consistency is achieved.

5. Beat together the buttermilk and egg, then add this mixture to the dry ingredients and mix lightly to form a lumpy batter.

6. Spoon evenly into the cake pan atop the apples, before smoothing the mixture by pressing gently downward while spreading, as to not unseat the bottom layer.

7. Bake for 30 to 35 minutes, or until a toothpick inserted into the center can be removed cleanly and the top reaches a golden brown.

8. Immediately free the sides of the cake with a sharp knife if needed, and invert onto a serving plate. Serve immediately with Chantilly cream or vanilla ice cream.

> **TIP FROM YESTERYEAR**
> This cake is best when served right out of the oven and eaten warm, as when it cools it will tend to become more moist in the center.

Blackberry Jam Cake

LAYER CAKE • 9-inch cake

Prep: 30 minutes
Cook: 40 minutes

CAKE

½ cup (115g) butter, softened

1 cup (200g) granulated sugar

Yolks of 3 large eggs, reserve whites

2 cups (280g) all-purpose flour

¾ tsp ground allspice

¼ tsp ground cloves

½ tsp salt

1 tsp baking soda

½ cup (115g) sour cream

1 cup (340g) blackberry jam, or seedless preserves

ERMINE FROSTING

1 cup (140g) all-purpose flour

1½ cups (300g) granulated sugar

2 cups (470ml) whole milk

1½ cups (340g) butter, softened and cubed

3 tsp vanilla extract

There are many ways to flavor a cake: chocolate, vanilla, spices, and such. But one very popular way that we, for whatever reason, now seem to pass by, is the use of fruit jams and preserves. So familiar was the jam cake in the 1920s, that most every community cookbook would have a recipe for one, and blackberry was often the choice. Preserves after all, keep very well, and the sweetness, moisture, and flavor that they can offer to a cake is uniquely suited to a fine result. This recipe combines the vintage jam method with an equally vintage and charming ermine frosting, and gives you a stately and fruity spice cake that stands out proudly among modern mainstays.

CAKE METHOD

1. Preheat the oven to 350°F (180°C). Grease two 9-inch (23-cm) cake pans.

2. Cream together the butter and sugar. Beat in the 3 egg yolks.

3. In a separate bowl, combine the flour, allspice, cloves, salt, and baking soda.

4. In a third bowl, whisk smooth the sour cream and the jam.

5. In the bowl of a stand mixer fitted with a whisk attachment, or in a fourth bowl with which an electric hand mixer is to be used, beat the reserved egg whites stiff.

6. Fold the dry ingredients into the creamed mixture alternately with the sour cream and jam mixture.

7. Working quickly, fold in the beaten egg whites in three additions.

8. Turn the batter into the prepared pans and bake for 35 to 40 minutes, or until a toothpick inserted into the center can be removed cleanly. Cool in the pans for 10 minutes before transferring to a wire rack to cool completely.

ERMINE FROSTING METHOD

9. In a large saucepan over medium heat, combine the flour and sugar by slowly whisking in the milk. Whisk until the mixture thickens, about 5 minutes.

10. Transfer to a heatproof bowl, and beat the mixture using a stand mixer or an electric hand mixer for 10 minutes. The mixture must be cool enough to not melt the butter. Slowly add in the cubed butter while beating. Beat until smooth.

11. Add the vanilla and beat for another 5 minutes until a fluffy, spreadable consistency is reached.

12. Spread the frosting evenly atop the first cake. Invert the second cake atop the filling to form the second layer.

13. Frost the assembled cake with the remaining frosting.

Continental Johnny Cake

CORNBREAD • 9-inch cornbread

Prep: 20 minutes
Cook: 25 minutes

1 large egg

½ cup (100g) granulated sugar

1 cup (235ml) whole milk, scalded and slightly cooled

⅓ cup (80ml) honey

¼ cup (60ml) vegetable oil, or melted lard

1 cup (140g) all-purpose flour

1 cup (122g) yellow cornmeal

2 tsp baking powder

1 tsp salt

1 tbsp butter

To say that I think one cornbread is superior to another is a surefire way to find myself a marked man in America. It is a polarizing and touchy subject, and many potluck brawls and erasures from wills have ensued from such inflammatory remarks. So though I may end up bound and gagged in the trunk of a Lincoln on some lonesome, urban shipping dock under the cover of darkness—I am still willing to say that I think the *Continental Johnny Cake* is the best cornbread. Period. It is worth speaking on the name Johnny Cake, as it means many things to many people depending on where you find yourself and when. In American cookbooks from the East Coast during the early 1920s, Johnny Cake most often denoted a cornbread of the sweet variety, sometimes even filled with apples or a spiced flavor. This recipe is simply a classic. Sweetened expertly with honey and crisped to a perfect caramelized gold by a cast-iron pan.

METHOD

1. Place a seasoned 9-inch (23-cm) cast iron skillet in the oven before preheating it to 400°F (205°C).

2. In a medium bowl, beat together the egg and granulated sugar with a whisk.

3. Mix in the scalded milk, honey, and vegetable oil.

4. In a separate large bowl, combine the flour, cornmeal, baking powder, and salt. Add the wet ingredients and mix until well combined.

5. When the oven is at temperature, carefully remove the hot skillet and add the butter to melt and coat the pan, ensuring the sides are well-coated.

6. Pour the batter into the skillet, and quickly return it to the oven to bake for 18 to 20 minutes. Alternatively, the batter may be baked in a greased 9-inch pie pan (not preheated in the oven) for 20 to 25 minutes.

7. Turn out onto a cutting board and serve warm.

Unemployment Pudding

PUDDING • 8 ramekins

Prep: 30 minutes
Cook: 20 minutes

PUDDING
¼ cup (55g) butter, softened
½ cup (100g) granulated sugar
2 tbsp maple syrup
Yolks of 2 large eggs
1½ cups (210g) all-purpose flour
½ tsp baking powder
¼ tsp baking soda
¾ cup (180ml) whole milk

SAUCE
¼ cup (55g) butter, softened
½ cup (120ml) whole milk
1⅓ cups (290g) packed dark
   brown sugar
½ cup (120ml) maple syrup

When factory workers found themselves jobless at the start of the Great Depression in 1929 Quebec, their resolve did not falter to the point of denying themselves a delectable dessert. Although a third of Canada's labor force was without work that year, and available ingredients were severely kneecapped, Canadians often had two things: dairy and maple syrup. So this dessert—known as Pouding Chomeur in French—runs with that, and features a lovely cake batter bathed in the cozy embrace of a maple sauce. It is a dessert that casts away the bitter cold of winter and wraps you in sweet bliss. It is a perfect example of how brilliant ideas can emerge from times of utter adversity.

PUDDING METHOD

1. Preheat the oven to 350°F (180°C).

2. In a large bowl, cream together the butter, sugar, and maple syrup until light and fluffy. Beat in the egg yolks. The mixture may look separated.

3. In a separate bowl, combine the flour, baking powder, and baking soda. Add to the creamed mixture alternately with the milk. Beat until no lumps remain. Set aside.

SAUCE METHOD

4. In a saucepan over high heat, mix together all the sauce ingredients and bring to a boil, stirring occasionally. Let boil for 5 minutes while you prepare the ramekins.

5. Grease 8 standard (5oz) ramekins, or other suitably sized oven-safe dishware, and place them atop a baking sheet. Evenly divide the prepared batter into them. This is best done with a scale.

6. Once the sauce mixture has reduced, carefully pour equal amounts atop the batter.

7. Bake for 15 to 20 minutes, or until a toothpick inserted into the center can be removed without crumbs. Serve warm.

Anadama Bread

YEAST BREAD • 9×5-inch loaf

Prep: 2 hours
Cook: 55 minutes

½ cup (85g) yellow cornmeal

⅓ cup (80ml) molasses

3 tbsp butter, softened

2 tsp salt

1 cup (235ml) boiling water

1 packet active dry yeast
   (2¼ tsp, 7g)

1 large egg, beaten

1 cup (140g) whole wheat flour

2 cups (280g) all-purpose flour

I don't find myself baking many traditional yeast breads. I have far too much of a sweet tooth and a desire for frostings and glazes. So I fear that if I had full control over the baking of a loaf, numerous artisan bread purists would escape from the local yoga studios and subject me to something horrid like a juice cleanse for my sacrilege. Despite my usual avoidance of plain breads, I found this old New England loaf absolutely wonderful. With its name and early varieties originating as far back as the 1890s, *Anadama Bread* was born in Rockport, Massachusetts. Legend has it that a fisherman had grown tired of his wife Anna's poorly made dinners of molasses and cornmeal. In frustration, he reached for a jar of flour and threw some in during a fitful effort to hopefully bake his porridge into something edible, yelling "Anna, damn her!" Although the story is likely legend alone, this bread certainly is not. The sweetness of yeast and molasses mingle perfectly with nutty corn and whole wheat flavors. This 1920s New England recipe makes things easy by letting you knead in the bowl, too!

METHOD

1. In a large heatproof bowl, combine the cornmeal, molasses, butter, and salt. Add in the boiling water, and stir until the butter has melted. Let the mixture stand until lukewarm (below 100°F/38°C).

2. Ensuring the mixture has cooled, stir in the yeast, and let stand for 5 minutes.

3. Add the beaten egg and whole wheat flour. Beat vigorously for 3 minutes.

4. Using your hands, add the all-purpose flour and knead in the bowl until a smooth ball is formed.

5. Cover the bowl and let rise for 30 to 40 minutes in a warm place.

6. Remove the dough from the bowl and knead briefly on the counter, forming a log shape roughly equal to the length of a loaf pan (9×5-inch/23×13-cm) keeping any seams on the bottom.

7. Transfer the dough to a greased loaf pan, smooth side up, and let rise in a warm place for 1 to 1½ hours. Dough should rise above the sides of the pan.

8. Bake at 350°F (180°C) for 45 to 55 minutes.

9. Transfer the bread to a wire rack immediately, and let cool completely before slicing.

Dates

Thumb through early 20th century cookbooks and you'll find one thing immediately apparent: Our forefathers and -mothers were utterly obsessed with dates. One would get the idea that if they couldn't get their fix, they'd rip off their bowler hats and petticoats in a moral panic and commit arson at the local soda fountain, and civil unrest would certainly ensue. I, too, am obsessed with dates. Behind men, they are my favorite fruit. Though they look vaguely like oversized cockroach eggs, their taste is incredibly rich and sweet. Indeed, the average date is about 70 percent sugar by weight, which in addition to being somewhat dried, allows them to have an impressively lengthy shelf life compared to other fruits.

Because of this, the date would finagle its way into every possible corner of baking by the midcentury: cookies, muffins, cakes, soufflés, dessert sauces, pastries, and fried goods. In 1930s to 1950s cookbooks, it would not be unusual for 7 out of 10 recipes in a dessert section to contain dates. I would kill for an equivalent modern adoration.

The sticky fruit came to the United States near the turn of the 20th century, when the US Department of Agriculture sent agricultural "explorers" across the globe in search of suitable, profitable crops that would flourish on American land. One of those explorers, Walter T. Swingle, brought back offshoots of a date palm he had gathered in Algeria. Dates have been grown and celebrated in the Middle East for centuries, and it just so happened that the Colorado Desert of Southern California perfectly mimicked the natural climate of the crop.

Planting began immediately, and by 1955, 48 million pounds of dates were being harvested annually in California alone, with more coming from the surrounding Mojave and Sonoran deserts. Dates saturated the American market, and found themselves cheaply on grocer's shelves from coast to coast, becoming a symbol of the Golden State's Coachella Valley in the process. Dates and their meaning to California are still celebrated today during the Riverside County Fair and National Date Festival every year in Indio.

Date Soufflé

BAKED DESSERT • 1½ quart casserole dish

Prep: 20 minutes
Cook: 40 minutes

SOUFFLÉ
2 tbsp butter, softened

3 tbsp sugar

Yolks of 3 large eggs,
    reserve whites

¾ cup (180ml) whole milk

¼ cup (35g) all-purpose flour

1 tsp salt

2⅔ cups (400g) chopped dates

ORANGE SAUCE
1 cup (200g) granulated sugar

1 cup (235ml) freshly squeezed
    orange juice

Zest of 1 large orange

Juice of 1 lemon

1 tbsp cornstarch

1 tbsp butter, softened

Yolk of 1 large egg

I'm intimidated by traditional soufflés. Like wild horses, they frighten me and are difficult to master. Luckily, this is not one of those soufflés. The date lovers of yesteryear have imbued their humble, homey warmth into this easy dessert to create a soft and delicate affair just begging to be served. Unrivaled date flavor and richness are wrapped here within a soft sponge, and in tandem with the bright pop of a simple orange sauce, it is nearly criminal in its decadence.

SOUFFLÉ METHOD

1. Preheat the oven to 350°F (180°C). Grease a 1½- or 2-quart (1.4-1.9L) casserole dish.

2. Cream together the butter and sugar until light and fluffy. Beat in the 3 egg yolks.

3. Add the milk alternately with the flour. Mix lightly.

4. In the bowl of a stand mixer fitted with a whisk attachment, or in a large bowl with which an electric hand mixer is to be used, beat the reserved egg whites and the salt to form stiff peaks. Fold into the creamed mixture in three additions.

5. Fold in the chopped dates.

6. Pour into the prepared dish. Set this casserole dish in a larger baking pan filled with enough boiling water to fill at least halfway up the casserole dish. It is best to fill the larger baking pan with water once on the oven grate, as to not risk spilling hot water.

7. Bake for 35 to 40 minutes.

ORANGE SAUCE METHOD

8. Combine all the sauce ingredients and cook in a double boiler until the mixture thickens, and coats the back of a spoon. Serve over portions of warm soufflé.

Date Bars

BAR • 8×8-inch pan

Prep: 20 minutes
Cook: 35 minutes

FILLING

1½ cups (225g) chopped dates
(One 8oz/227g package)

⅔ cup (160ml) water

¾ cup (150g) granulated sugar

Juice of 1 lemon

CRUST

1½ cups (210g) all-purpose flour

1 cup (220g) packed dark
brown sugar

1 cup (90g) rolled oats

¾ cup (170g) butter, cold and
cubed

1 large egg, beaten, for egg
wash

The most famed of the date baked goods is arguably the *Date Bar*. Throughout the majority of the 20th century, these bars were in nearly every rural cookbook, served at each corner diner, and whenever company came knocking they'd be atop the coffee table in an instant. The *Date Bar* is the brownie of old, and was positively ubiquitous from the late 1910s right up to the 1970s. This recipe is of the type you would find in the early 1950s: A crunchy, cookie-like crust below a gooey date center, all nestled beneath a crisp oat topping. Good through simplicity, defined.

FILLING METHOD

1. In a small saucepan over medium heat, combine the filling ingredients and bring to a boil, stirring occasionally. Boil until significantly thickened and syrupy, about 10 minutes.

CRUST & ASSEMBLY METHOD

2. Preheat the oven to 350°F (180°C).

3. In a large bowl, combine the flour, brown sugar, oats, and butter. Rub the dry mixture into the butter with your fingers until the mixture is a uniform consistency like wet sand, and no large lumps of butter remain. Divide the mixture in half.

4. Firmly press half the crumbs into the bottom and partway up the sides of an 8×8-inch (20×20-cm) pan. Gently pour and spread the filling over this crust layer.

5. Spread the remaining crumbs evenly atop the filling. Pack gently. Brush the beaten egg as best you can over the top crust.

6. Bake for 30 to 35 minutes, until the top turns a golden brown and the sides begin to darken. Cool completely in the pan before cutting into bars.

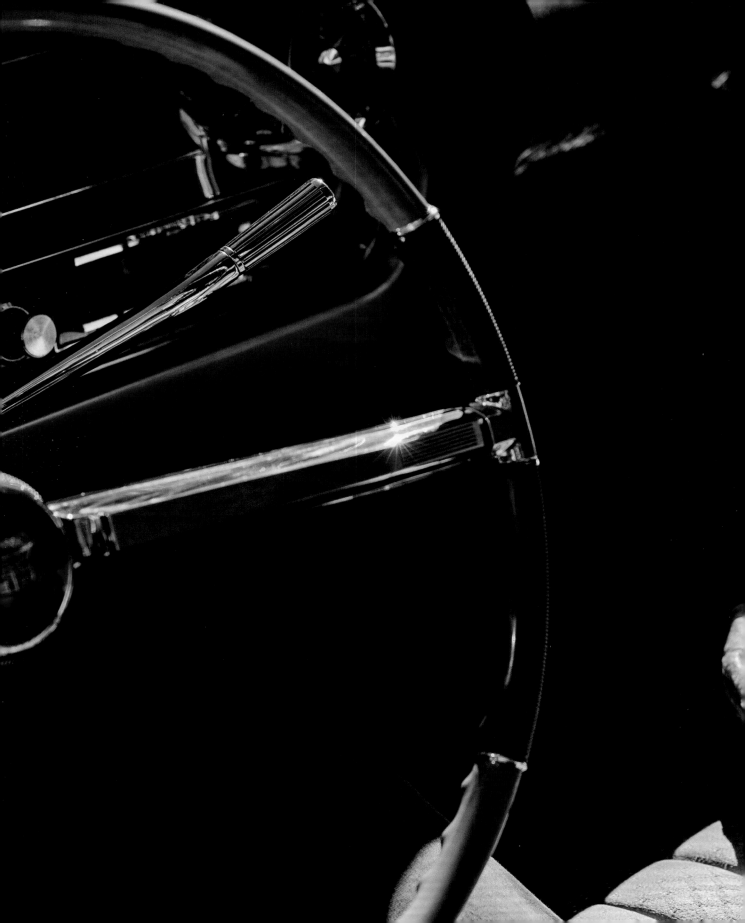

Date Macaroons

MACAROON • 1 dozen

Prep: 20 minutes
Cook: 22 minutes

1 heaping cup (150g) whole
  filberts or hazelnuts, skins
  removed
Whites of 2 large eggs
½ tsp vanilla extract
1 cup (120g) powdered sugar
1 cup (150g) chopped dates

There was divine intervention at work when the first person thought to pair dates with filberts, and even further brilliance when they were joined together within the crisp shell and chewy center of a macaroon. *Date Macaroons* found themselves quite popular in the 1940s, where they were either the sole add-in, or paired with walnuts or pecans. This recipe is my favorite iteration from that era. I do not suggest skipping the toasting of the filberts—that's where these macaroons really shine.

METHOD

1. Preheat the oven to 350°F (180°C).

2. Place filberts on a baking sheet, and toast for 10 minutes. Remove and let cool before chopping the nuts, or crushing them with the bottom of a glass.

3. In the bowl of a stand mixer fitted with a whisk attachment, or in a large bowl with which an electric hand mixer is to be used, beat the egg whites stiff before beating in the vanilla.

4. Gradually fold in the powdered sugar. The mixture will deflate.

5. Fold in the chopped dates and chopped filberts.

6. Drop by rounded tablespoon or cookie scoop onto a parchment-lined or greased baking sheet.

7. Bake for 18 to 22 minutes, or until macaroons take on a light golden color.

8. Cool completely on the baking sheet and store in an airtight container.

Date Nut Loaf

QUICKBREAD • 9×5-inch loaf

**Prep: 15 minutes
Cook: 1 hour**

---

1 cup (235ml) boiling water

1 cup (150g) chopped dates

½ cup (115g) butter, softened

1 cup (200g) granulated sugar

2 large eggs

2 cups (280g) all-purpose flour

1 tsp baking soda

½ tsp ground cinnamon

1 cup (115g) chopped walnuts

It might be difficult for modern folks to fathom a time when banana bread was not the people's favorite quickbread. But indeed, before the 1970s that title went to the noble *Date Nut Loaf*, or date bread. It is a quintessential quickbread of yesteryear, and it still peeks its head above the obscurity line during Christmastime, if you find yourself in the United Kingdom. Deep date flavor, a moist crumb, and the simple marvel of well-formed crust awaits should you bake this classic loaf.

METHOD

1. Preheat the oven to 350°F (180°C). Grease a 9×5-inch (23×13-cm) loaf pan.

2. Pour boiling water over the chopped dates and let stand for at least 5 minutes. Do not drain.

3. In a large bowl, cream together the butter and sugar until light and fluffy. Beat in the eggs.

4. In a separate bowl, combine the flour, baking soda, and cinnamon. Add to the creamed mixture alternately with the dates and their water. Mix until barely combined.

5. Fold in the chopped walnuts.

6. Turn into the prepared pan and bake for roughly 55 to 65 minutes, or until a toothpick inserted into the center can be removed cleanly.

7. Cool in the pan for 10 minutes before inverting onto a wire rack to cool completely. A sharp knife may be run along the edges should the loaf stick.

TIP FROM YESTERYEAR
For a more Christmas-suitable Date Nut Loaf, substitute the granulated sugar with dark brown sugar, and use ¾ cups (180ml) boiling water with ¼ cup (60ml) molasses or treacle added to the dates with step 2. Bake the same.

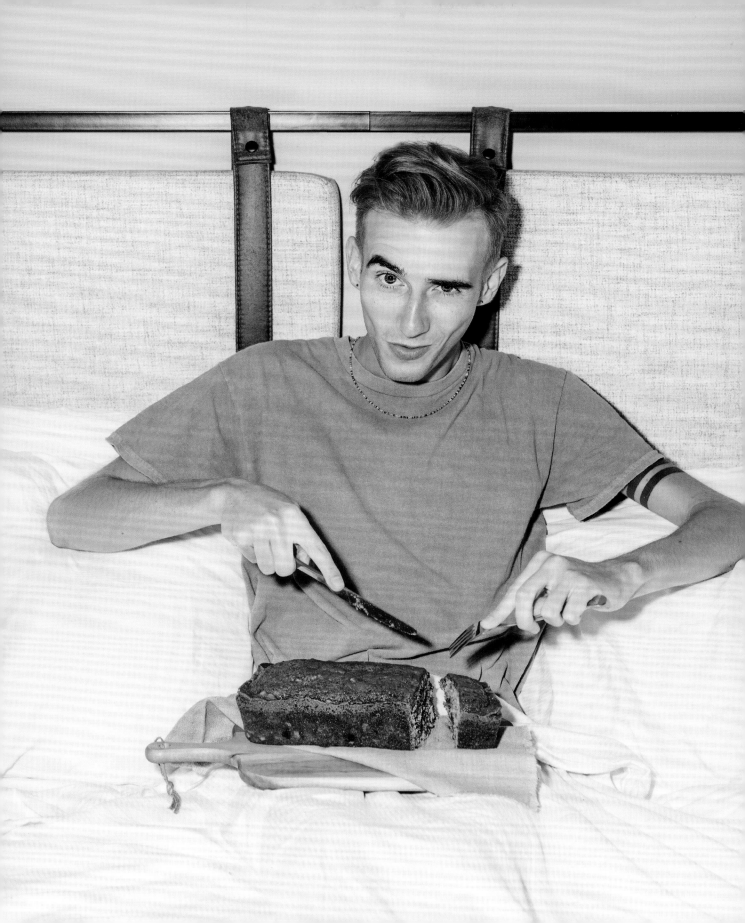

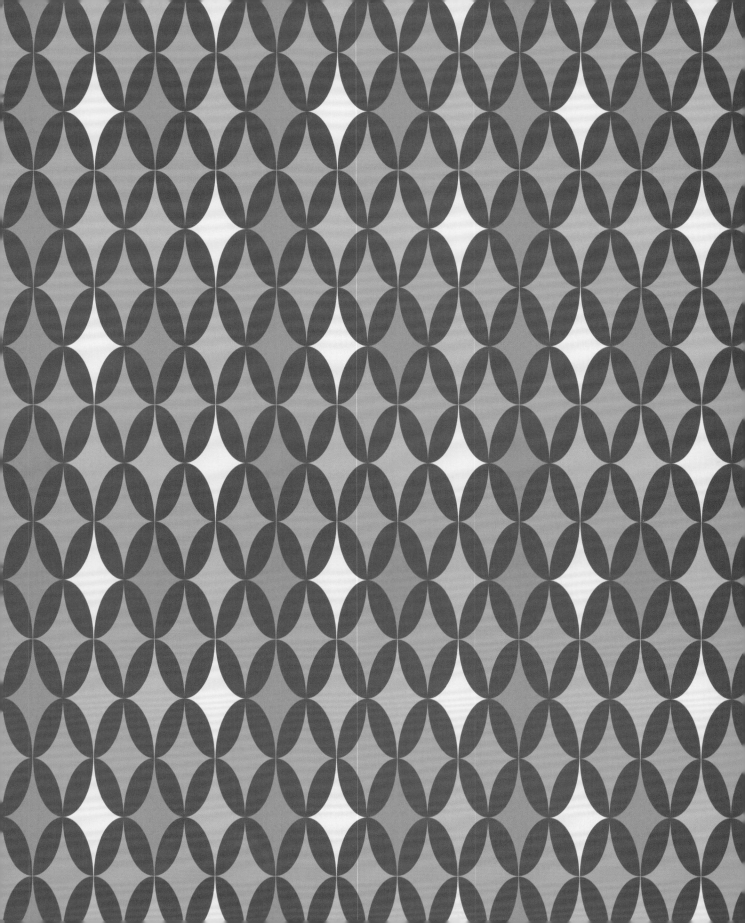

1930s

The rigors and hardships of the Great Depression were not kind to the world of baking during the 1930s. A severely kneecapped ability to obtain many of the standard baker's ingredients made dessert truly a rare occurrence for a great many people.

Skyrocketing unemployment and low household funds meant that the focus was no longer on what flavor cake could be made, but whether or not the family could avoid hunger. For those better off, like residents of more rural and farming communities, baked goods could still continue to be enjoyed quite regularly, and indeed these are the areas where most of the recipes of this section originate from. It is important to note that the experience and response to the Depression was not uniform across the populace.

The Depression was not confined to the US; and Great Britain found its own difficulties dealing with the financial crisis. In addition, the tension in Europe leading up to the start of World War II implored the public to conserve and reduce extraneous consumption long before rationing even began in the 1940s, making towering cakes and sparkling pies at local gatherings a somewhat tepid sight.

Despite this, the wealthy folks of the time might not have even known the Great Depression was occurring if it weren't for the press. And they were eager to snatch up the new-fangled and expensive appliances like home refrigerators to aid their servants in producing colorful, magnificent spreads of baked goods on a new level.

Icebox Pinwheels

COOKIE • 2 dozen

Prep: 5 hours
Cook: 10 minutes

½ cup (115g) butter, softened

½ cup (100g) granulated sugar

Yolk of 1 large egg

2 tsp vanilla extract

1¾ cups (245g) all-purpose
 flour

½ tsp salt

2 tbsp whole milk

1oz (28g) unsweetened
 chocolate, melted

Sometimes you want a cookie that looks like it's been made by somebody who knows what they're doing. Luckily for us, the widespread adoption of home refrigerators (colloquially called iceboxes) in the 1930s gave rise to icebox cookies, a class of cookie which, among other benefits, allowed distinct patterns, cute shapes, and interesting designs to survive through the baking process. Thoroughly chilled dough after all, spreads and rises minimally. This recipe is a great sugar cookie dough, made infinitely more fun and tastier by a chocolate pinwheel spiraling throughout.

METHOD

1. Cream together the butter and sugar until light and fluffy. Beat in the egg yolk and vanilla.

2. Combine the flour and salt before adding to the creamed mixture alternately with the milk.

3. Divide the dough in half, and to one half, thoroughly blend in the melted chocolate. To create a uniform color, the hands might be used to mix. Chilling the dough briefly in the refrigerator will make the next step easier.

4. Roll each dough out on a floured surface to rectangles roughly 10×12 inches (25×30cm) in size. Trim any unsightly edges to ensure they are the same size.

5. Carefully place the plain dough atop the chocolate dough, slightly offset, such that one longer edge of the plain dough extends beyond that of the chocolate by about a half inch (1cm).

6. Starting at the edge opposite the overhang, roll lengthwise evenly and tightly like a jelly roll. Wrap in wax paper and chill overnight, or for a minimum of 4 hours.

7. Preheat the oven to 350°F (180°C). Using a sharp knife, slice thinly (¼ inch), wiping the knife after each cut, and place the cookies cut side down on a greased or parchment-lined cookie sheet. This should yield 24 cookies.

8. Bake for 8 to 10 minutes. Cool briefly on the baking sheet before transferring to a wire rack to cool completely.

Rocks

BISCUIT • 1 dozen

Prep: 20 minutes
Cook: 18 minutes

1¾ cup (245g) all-purpose flour

½ cup (115g) vegetable shortening, lard, or butter, cold and cubed

½ cup (100g) granulated sugar

1 large egg

1 tbsp orange zest

2–3 tbsp whole milk

1 cup (160g) raisins, currants, golden raisins, or any combination of the three

Coarse grained sugar, for sprinkling

I assure you that you won't be needing a dentist to eat these. No, these are a classic tea-time bun once promoted by the British Ministry of Food during World War II. They were to be made easily during wartime rationing with dried egg powder and any drippings you may have had lying around. The Commonwealth calls them rock cakes, or rock buns, but in typical American fashion, the name was often (and comically) shortened to *Rocks* in many US cookbooks. These are the scones of rough times, but I do not think they should be considered any lesser. Easily prepared, and imbued with a light flavor of orange—you will feel thankful as you tear them open to be buttered.

METHOD

1. Preheat the oven to 375°F (190°C).

2. In a large bowl, combine the flour and the shortening. Rub the flour into the shortening with your fingers until the mixture is a uniform consistency, like breadcrumbs.

3. Using a wooden spoon, mix in the sugar, egg, and orange zest. Begin to add the milk a tablespoon at a time, until a thick, sticky dough is formed.

4. Mix in the dried fruit.

5. Drop in rough 3-tablespoon portions onto a parchment-lined baking sheet.

6. Sprinkle with coarse grained sugar and bake for 15 to 18 minutes, until the buns take a rich golden color. Leave to cool on the baking sheet. Enjoy warm with butter.

Peanut Butter Bread

QUICKBREAD · 9×5-inch loaf

Prep: 20 minutes
Cook: 1 hour

2 cups (280g) all-purpose flour

½ tsp salt

4 tsp baking powder (use 2 ¼
 tsp if baking at or above
 5,000 feet)

¼ cup (50g) granulated sugar

1⅓ cup (315ml) whole milk

½ cup (135g) peanut butter

"So good from so little," was my reaction when I first tried this Great Depression *Peanut Butter Bread* on camera in 2021. It has since become one of the most beloved recipes I've explored. When eggs, butter, and sugar were scarce during the height of the crisis, especially in urban centers, home economists found themselves lacking the foundational ingredients to make nearly any cake or quickbread. However, shelf-stable, affordable, and available jarred peanut butter offered a solution: Needed fat for texture and moisture, emulsifiers for a good crumb, nuttiness for flavor, and a touch of sweetness—it was a perfect marriage of problem and solution. This recipe is true to its 1932 roots, and it not only tastes beautiful (especially when buttered), but is utterly simple to make.

METHOD

1. Preheat the oven to 350°F (180°C). Grease a 9×5-inch (23×13-cm) loaf pan.

2. In a large bowl, combine the flour, salt, baking powder, and sugar.

3. Mix in the milk and the peanut butter until well combined.

4. Turn into the prepared pan and bake for 55 to 65 minutes, or until a toothpick inserted into the center can be removed cleanly.

5. Cool in the pan for 10 minutes before transferring to a wire rack to cool completely.

Wacky Cake

CAKE • 8×8-inch cake

Prep: 15 minutes
Cook: 30 minutes

CAKE
1½ cups (210g) all-purpose flour
1 cup (200g) granulated sugar
⅓ cup (40g) cocoa powder
½ tsp salt
1 tsp baking soda
⅓ cup (80ml) vegetable oil
1 tsp vanilla extract
1 tbsp white vinegar
1 cup (235ml) water

FROSTING
1 cup (120g) powdered sugar
2 tbsp cocoa powder
Roughly 3 tbsp water

This is a Great Depression cake without butter, eggs, or milk. It is also a very good cake. These two things should not be concurrently true, and yet you, too, can experience the truth in about an hour's time. Known either as a wacky or a crazy cake, there are a few hypotheses on how it earned its name: one highlights surprise on how frugal decisions to omit eggs and replace milk with water and butter with oil could ever create a good result. The other is based on its peculiar and largely nonsensical method of mixing: making the batter in the pan, creating three wells, and filling them with the liquid ingredients before mixing with a fork. No matter the reasoning or the name, this is one of the best plain chocolate cakes around, and that's before you top it with a delightful chocolate glaze aimed to please your double-chocolate desires. There is a reason the *Wacky Cake* is still made to this day, and maybe that reason lies in the funny mixing.

CAKE METHOD

1. Preheat the oven to 350°F (180°C).

2. Directly in a ceramic or glass 8×8-inch (20×20-cm) baking dish, combine the flour, sugar, cocoa powder, salt, and baking soda. Mix until uniform.

3. Create three wells in the dry mixture, and into these wells add the vegetable oil, vanilla, and vinegar respectively so that each well contains a different ingredient.

4. Pour the water over the entire mixture and quickly whisk smooth using a fork or a whisk.

5. Bake for 25 to 30 minutes, or until a toothpick inserted into the center can be removed cleanly. Allow to cool completely in the pan, placed upon a wire rack.

FROSTING METHOD

6. In a small bowl, combine the powdered sugar and cocoa powder.

7. Slowly stir in the water until a thick, pourable consistency is reached. When the mixture is smooth, pour over the cooled cake. Cut into squares in the pan.

TIP FROM YESTERYEAR
If using a metal 8×8-inch baking dish, simply combine all the dry ingredients in a large bowl, and add the remaining liquid ingredients at once. Mix until smooth and pour into a greased pan. Bake the same.

Whipped Cream Cake

CAKE • 10-inch Bundt

Prep: 30 minutes
Cook: 1 hour

---

3 cups (420g) all-purpose flour

2¼ cups (450g) granulated
   sugar

3 tsp baking powder

Whites of 4 large eggs

¾ tsp salt

1½ cups (355ml) heavy cream,
   well chilled

2 tsp vanilla extract

¾ cup (180ml) water

Fresh berries, to serve

Whipped cream, to serve

Angel food cakes are not something you'd want to be making during a war—there are far more pressing matters, and you should likely find a weapon. Truly, the angel foods were especially unfit for service in the rationed home-front kitchen as they were wasteful and hormonal things, requiring obnoxious amounts of egg whites and masterful baking precision. So, during the start of WWII, the *Whipped Cream Cake* began to take hold as a cheat-method to create a cake similar to the angel food cake, using instead one quarter of the egg whites. Fluffy, rich, and luxurious is this vanilla cake. Halfway between angel food and a pound cake, this is the ultimate pairing with fresh fruit, Chantilly cream, or simply . . . your mouth. The *Whipped Cream Cake* is a perfect example of how scarcity and inventiveness go hand in hand, and the result is, in my opinion, better than the product our past generations were trying to mimic.

METHOD

1. Preheat the oven to 350°F (180°C). Grease a 10-inch (25-cm) tube or Bundt pan.

2. In a medium bowl, sift together the flour, sugar, and baking powder.

3. In the bowl of a stand mixer fitted with a whisk attachment, or in a large bowl with which an electric hand mixer is to be used, beat the egg whites and salt to stiff peaks.

4. In another large bowl, whip the chilled cream to stiff peaks using a stand mixer or an electric hand mixer.

5. Fold the egg whites into the whipped cream in three additions, before folding in the vanilla.

6. Add the dry ingredients into the egg white and cream mixture slowly. Alternate in turn with the water, ensuring the mixture does not get too stiff, nor too loose while folding.

7. Turn into the prepared pan, and bake for 50 to 60 minutes, or until a toothpick inserted into the center can be removed cleanly.

8. Cool in the pan for 10 minutes before inverting onto a wire rack to cool completely. Serve with fresh berries and whipped cream.

Mock Apple Pie

PIE • 9-inch pie

Prep: 40 minutes
Cook: 35 minutes
Cool: 2 hours

2 cups (400g) granulated sugar

2 cups (470ml) water

3 tsp cream of tartar

Juice of 1 lemon

40 Ritz crackers

1 double-crust pie pastry,
   (page 24)

1 tsp ground cinnamon

3 tbsp butter, cold and cut into
   thin pats

1 large egg

2 tbsp water

TIP FROM YESTERYEAR
With enough time the pie will solidify on its own without the fridge; and refrigerating it while still warm will cause a soggy mess.

There's no getting around it, this is a very weird one. This mock, or fake, apple pie manages to conjure an apple pie taste and texture from little more than butter crackers, sugar, and lemons. You'd think this would work about as well as trying to open a wine bottle with a pool noodle, but once again the dark baker's magic is at play. The *Mock Apple Pie* was scarcely known before the Depression. A few recipes using the name dotted southern United States cookbooks before the turn of the 20th century, and they used stale bread or soda crackers, but they were not well regarded for their accurate approximation. No, it wasn't until Nabisco's Ritz butter crackers were released in 1934, coinciding with sky-high apple prices at the hand of the Great Depression, that the *Mock Apple Pie* became known. Nabisco later jumped in on the phenomenon and began printing their own recipe on the back of Ritz boxes for all to enjoy, and the pie has since become one of the most well-known novelty recipes of yesteryear. It's more than a novelty, it's a good pie—and its ability to fool its eaters into thinking they're consuming apples is absolutely golden.

METHOD

1. Preheat the oven to 425°F (220°C).

2. In a large saucepan, combine the sugar, water, and cream of tartar over high heat, stirring occasionally. Once it boils, reduce heat to medium and boil for 20 minutes. Remove from heat, stir in the lemon juice, and allow to cool.

3. In a separate bowl, crush the Ritz crackers. Some large pieces are desired.

4. Fit your prepared bottom crust in a standard 9-inch (23-cm)pan (not a deep pie pan), and evenly place the crushed crackers inside. Pour the syrup mixture over the crackers before evenly sprinkling the ground cinnamon over the pie. Dot this filling with the pats of butter. Place the top crust over the pie and trim any excess. Seal and crimp the edges with a fork. Cut small slits in the top crust.

5. Beat the egg and water together to create an egg wash. Brush this over the top and edges of the pie.

6. Bake for 10 minutes, before reducing the temperature to 350° (180°C) for another 20 to 25 minutes, until the crust takes on a golden color. Let the pie cool to room temperature and solidify on a wire rack for 2 hours before serving. Pie may be refrigerated after this point before serving.

Potato Doughnuts

DOUGHNUT • 5 dozen

Prep: 1 hour 30 minutes
Cook: 20 minutes

---

2 medium-size russet potatoes

¼ cup (55g) butter, melted

3 large eggs

1¼ cups (250g) sugar

1 packet active dry yeast (2¼ tsp/7g) dissolved in ¼ cup (60ml) lukewarm water

4-5 cups (560g-700g) all-purpose flour

1 tsp ground nutmeg

1½ tsp salt

4 tsp baking powder

1 tsp baking soda

¾ cup (180ml) buttermilk

½ tsp vanilla extract

Canola, coconut, or peanut oil, for frying

1 cup (200g) granulated sugar, to 4 tbsp ground cinnamon, for coating

I seldom trust anybody who doesn't yield to a good doughnut every now and then. I also don't trust anyone who spells doughnut as donut. It seems I trust very few people. But I do trust in this recipe's ability to show you how good a doughnut the power of the potato can create. This spudnut recipe is all the things you love about a classic yeast doughnut, but with an added je ne sais quoi from the potato starches, buttermilk, the trifecta of leavening, and a simple cinnamon-sugar coating. These aren't your grandfather's doughnuts, they're your great-great-grandfather's doughnuts, and he's glad you've been made aware of them.

METHOD

1. Wash, peel, and dice the raw potatoes. In a medium saucepan over high heat, add water to cover and boil until fork tender. Drain, mash, and measure out 1 cup.

2. In a very large bowl, add the mashed potato and the melted butter. Beat very well.

3. In a separate bowl, whisk together the eggs and the sugar. Add this to the potato mixture and beat well.

4. Stir in the yeast and water mixture.

5. In a third bowl, combine the flour, nutmeg, salt, baking powder, and baking soda. Combine the buttermilk and vanilla. Alternate adding the dry ingredients and buttermilk mixture to the potato mixture.

6. Cover the mixing bowl with a clean kitchen towel and let stand for an hour.

7. Dust a worktop liberally with flour. Turn out the dough, and roll evenly to a half-inch thickness. Cut with a floured doughnut cutter.

8. In a large, heavy-bottomed pot or Dutch oven, add oil to a depth of 2 inches (5cm) and heat to 375°F (190°C)

9. Fry the doughnuts in small batches until golden brown on each side. About 2 minutes per side. Set on a wire rack topped with paper towels.

10. Coat the doughnuts in the cinnamon sugar while still warm.

TIP FROM YESTERYEAR
Your leftover doughnut holes are just as tasty! You can fry them just the same as the doughnuts. Flipping them until golden all around. About 2 minutes total.

Baked Apples

BAKED FRUIT • 4 apples

Prep: 20 minutes
Cook: 1 hour

4 large apples, Honeycrisp or
   Gala
½ cup (100g) granulated sugar
5 tsp ground cinnamon
¼ cup (25g) rolled oats
4 tbsp (55g) butter, softened

When cold nights befall your town's homesteads and main streets, and you pine for the cozy warmth of cinnamon-spice and apple to abate winter's descent, this easy Great Depression dessert of *Baked Apples* will be your savior. It is so easy that a stray newspaper on an abandoned street corner would likely be able to execute its preparation flawlessly. Which makes the incredible result of warm, tender apples, spiced and sweetened beneath a light, oaty crunch all the more impressive.

METHOD

1. Preheat the oven to 375°F (190°C). Line a 2-quart (1.9L) casserole dish or a 9×9-inch (23×23-cm) baking pan with aluminum foil.

2. Core (but do not peel) the apples, taking care not to pierce through the bottom. Place the apples, cored side up, into the prepared pan.

3. In a small bowl, combine the sugar, cinnamon, and rolled oats. Heap and compress this mixture into the cored apples. Place 1 tablespoon (15g) of butter per apple atop the sugar mixture.

4. Pour enough water into the baking dish as to fill roughly 1 inch (3cm) from the bottom.

5. Bake for 60 to 70 minutes, or until the apples are tender and look a bit dreary.

Potato Candy

CONFECTION • 24 pieces

Prep: 1 hour 40 minutes
Cook: None

1 small russet potato
6–7½ cups (720–900g)
  powdered sugar
1 jar (16.3oz/462g) peanut
  butter

One of the most beloved of the homestyle midwestern American confections is *Potato Candy*—and it's positively mad. A month's supply of powdered sugar with a bit of mashed potato gives birth to a scrumptious fondant, and all it begs for is a layer of peanut butter to complete its transformation into a swirled yuletide treat so surprisingly moreish that it will take you aback. When I first made *Potato Candy* I could not stop laughing at the particular, yet humble ridiculousness of its execution, but that laughter quickly turned to joy when I understood that outstanding confectionery can come from homegrown inventiveness alone.

METHOD

1. Wash, peel, and dice the raw potato. In a small saucepan over high heat, add water to cover and boil until fork tender. Drain, mash, and measure out ½ cup. Place in a very large bowl and allow to cool completely to room temperature.

2. Begin beating in the powdered sugar, 1 cup at a time. After the sixth cup, the dough should be firm enough to roll into a ball. If it isn't, additional powdered sugar may be added. The dough needs to be firm enough to be rolled effectively.

3. Wrap dough and refrigerate for 40 to 60 minutes. Over-chilling will result in it being brittle.

4. Divide the dough in half, and on a surface liberally dusted with powdered sugar, roll one half to a rectangle of ⅓-inch (1-cm) thickness. Trim any unsightly edges.

5. Evenly spread the peanut butter over the surface, leaving a ½-inch border around the perimeter.

6. Carefully roll lengthwise (starting at a longer edge) to form a log.

7. Repeat the shaping and rolling process with the other half of the dough.

8. Cut formed logs to ½-inch thick disks using a sharp knife. Chilling the logs might be required to make this process easier. Store refrigerated in an airtight container.

TIP FROM YESTERYEAR
Potato candy is very sticky when being rolled, so don't skip dusting your worktop with powdered sugar. You can line your counter with parchment paper and dust the paper with powdered sugar for even less mess!

Banana Marlow

ICE CREAM • 1¼ quarts

Prep: 3 hours
Cook: None

32 marshmallows or
  4 cups (200g) of mini
  marshmallows

¾ cup (180ml) whole milk

Juice of 1 lemon

1 cup (250g) mashed bananas

1 tsp vanilla extract

1½ cups (355ml) heavy cream

½ cup (85g) chopped
  maraschino cherries

The passage of time is unforgiving, as it allows marvelous things to fade into obscurity. Thankfully, it allows the embarrassing things we do in life to fade as well. Like the time I accidentally called a waitress "Mom," or fell for my straight friend. The marlow, however, is not embarrassing, it is an entire class of ice cream that was once popular during the early half of the 20th century. Whereby gelatos are milk and cream based, and sorbets are more water and fruit based, the marlow stands proud to be marshmallow based. This homemade marlow of sweet banana, bright maraschino cherries, and vanilla-marshmallow flavors tastes of all the good things vintage. It is gay, light, and beautifully kitschy. The key here is to take the time to disturb the mixture every 40 minutes or so during the initial freezing process, something home ice cream makers will be familiar with, to avoid too firm a texture. Of course, if you have an ice-cream machine, there is nothing wrong with making use of it here.

METHOD

1. In a medium saucepan over low heat, melt the marshmallows in the milk. Stirring occasionally until uniform.

2. Add the lemon juice and the mashed bananas. Remove from heat, stir in the vanilla, and transfer to a large heatproof bowl to cool completely to room temperature.

3. In the bowl of a stand mixer fitted with a whisk attachment, or in a large bowl with which an electric hand mixer is to be used, whip the heavy cream until smooth, stiff peaks are formed, but do not whip beyond this point.

4. Fold the whipped cream into the cooled marshmallow mixture in three additions. Fold gently until uniform.

5. Fold in the chopped maraschino cherries.

6. Transfer the marlow into a 9×13-inch (23×33-cm) shallow casserole dish. Cover and freeze.

7. For a smoother marlow, agitate the mixture every 40 minutes by stirring and pulling the freezing edges of the mixture inward. Repeat three to four times. Allow at least 30 minutes to partially thaw before serving.

1940s

Like many recreations during the worldwide turbulence of the 1940s, the hobby of baking took its position on the back burner. It was difficult to justify spreads of towering cakes, plentiful sweets, and beautiful desserts during a time of ingredient scarcity.

Sugar, the baker's most trusted confidant, was heavily rationed in the United States from 1942 to 1946, during which time Americans had to wrestle with only half the sugar they were previously accustomed to per week. Of course, this was a major setback for the field of dentistry as a whole, whose practitioners must've suddenly and frustratingly found themselves without work, but it did not spell the end of bakery, for where there is a will, there is a way.

The baked goods of the 1940s reflected the make-do attitudes of wartime rationing, national pride through patriotism, and an eventual return to the usual home baker's antics once the war was over. Victory celebrations across the United Kingdom and the United States saw jubilant block parties and gatherings aplenty, where abundant cakes, cookies, and desserts marked an end to the stalwart adherence to conserving foodstuffs. With new cavities to fill, even our friends the dentists were once again swinging from the rafters with joy.

The scarcities had reignited appreciation for all things sweet, the dessert became a symbol of overcoming, and people had more reason than ever to bake with heart and soul. The recipes in this section highlight good-old fashioned baking, clever adaptations to ingredient shortages, and different perspectives.

Peanut Butter Styrofoams

MACAROON • 1 dozen

Prep: 20 minutes
Cook: 22 minutes

Whites of 2 large eggs
¾ cup (150g) granulated sugar
½ cup (135g) peanut butter

Usually, a compulsion to eat Styrofoam would be considered a medical issue, and about halfway through the list of worthy reasons for institutionalization. However, this macaroon has a delightful sense of humor as it makes you do just that—compulsively want to eat Styrofoam. These macaroons are a dead simple concept and a fantastic take on a truly different peanut butter cookie. A sweet and crispy shell with a hollow center comes before a quaint chew of peanut-buttery goodness. They are a quirky experience in the mouth, there's no denying it—but how could you deny these?

METHOD

1. Preheat the oven to 325°F (165°C).

2. In the bowl of a stand mixer fitted with a whisk attachment, or in a large bowl with which an electric hand mixer is to be used, beat the egg whites to stiff peaks, before gradually adding in the granulated sugar 2 tablespoons at a time while beating. Beat until stiff, glossy peaks are formed.

3. In a separate bowl, beat the peanut butter to soften it before folding into the egg white mixture. Leaving some streaks of peanut butter is desired.

4. Drop by level tablespoon or small cookie scoop onto a parchment-lined baking sheet and bake for 20 to 22 minutes.

5. Cool completely on the baking sheet and store in an airtight container.

Dream Bars

BAR • 9×9-inch pan

Prep: 25 minutes
Cook: 20 minutes

CRUST

1 cup (140g) all-purpose flour

¼ cup (55g) packed light brown sugar

¼ cup (55g) butter, melted

TOP LAYER

2 large eggs

1 cup (220g) packed light brown sugar

2 tbsp all-purpose flour

½ tsp baking powder

1 tsp salt

1 cup (115g) finely chopped pecans

1 cup (140g) sweetened shredded coconut

The name of this bake is not hyperbole in the slightest. My first encounter with *Dream Bars* was transformative. A simplistic recipe with a wildly disproportionate result: they are outright dreamy. A crunchy cookie base holds up a soft, brown-sugar caramel chew interspersed with hits of coconut and nutty bites. I have yet to taste anything quite like them. Bar cookies like this one really began to take off in the 1940s, and were popular additions to tea-time plates and coffee tables. You might imagine a dream bar delicately placed besides a demitasse cup in a 1940s living room, patiently waiting to be eaten amid the sound of big band jazz. You, for one, needn't be so patient.

CRUST METHOD

1. Preheat the oven to 375°F (190°C).

2. In a medium bowl, combine the crust ingredients and mix until a uniform crumb is formed. Press this into the bottom and partway up the sides of a 9×9-inch (23×23-cm) pan.

3. Bake for 15 minutes. Remove the pan from the oven and let cool on a wire rack.

TOP LAYER METHOD

4. In a large bowl, beat together the eggs and brown sugar until smooth.

5. Thoroughly mix in the remaining ingredients in the order given.

6. Pour the mixture atop the baked bottom layer, and bake for 20 minutes. Transfer to a wire rack to cool completely in the pan. Once cold, cut to squares.

Oatmeal Honey Bread

QUICKBREAD • 9×5-inch loaf

Prep: 30 minutes
Cook: 50 minutes

1 cup (235ml) honey

½ cup (120ml) water

½ cup (115g) butter, softened

¼ cup (55g) packed dark brown
   sugar

1½ cups (135g) rolled oats

1¾ cups (245g) all-purpose
   flour

1 tsp baking soda

1 tsp salt

1 tsp ground cinnamon

1 large egg, beaten

Oatmeal breads were once in high fashion, both in traditional and quickbread forms. Associated most with dentures, oatmeal is distinctly old-fashioned, but that does not mean its use in breads is any less warranted. Here, the nuttiness oats can offer the world of baking—and the overall popularity of oatmeal breads pre-1940—was given a makeover with the glorious addition of honey. This recipe is among many similar ones put to the populace in the 1940s and 1950s through marketing leaflets from honey companies, assuring the consumer that honey could, and should, be used in your kitchen whenever possible. Some of their advertisement recipes were far-fetched, but others like this struck a perfect flavor combo. Nutty, sweet, moist, and rich, this quickbread is a hearty addition to your roster.

METHOD

1. Preheat the oven to 350°F (180°C). Grease a 9×5-inch (23×13-cm) loaf pan.

2. In a saucepan, combine the honey, water, butter, and brown sugar over medium heat. Bring to a simmer, but not a rolling boil. Remove from the heat and stir in the oats. Let stand for 10 minutes

3. In a large bowl, combine the flour, baking soda, salt, and cinnamon. Then pour in the cooled honey mixture and mix until barely combined

4. Add the egg and beat well for 30 seconds. Quickly turn into the prepared pan and bake for 45 to 50 minutes, or until a toothpick inserted into the center can be removed cleanly. Cool in pan for 10 minutes before transferring to a wire rack to cool completely.

5. Optionally, the bread may be removed from the loaf pan, put onto a baking sheet, and brushed with honey immediately after baking, before being returned to the oven for 2 minutes at 400°F (205°C) to create a honey glaze.

Leftover Bread Pancakes

PANCAKE • 8 pancakes

Prep: 15 minutes
Cook: 20 minutes

7-8 slices (220g) of sandwich
 bread, stale

1 cup (235ml) whole milk

¼ tsp salt

2 tbsp granulated sugar

1 tsp baking powder

1 large egg, beaten

I am obsessed with these pancakes. Despite the difficult times that led to their inception—limited pantry items, and the use of stale bread to approximate a favorite breakfast staple—I still reach for this recipe over others even in modern times of plenty. This 1940s make-do recipe proves that flour and traditional batters are not needed to create the wonderfully fluffy, and crispy pancakes that we love so much. It's also a benefit that I find this method far easier and more replicable than other pancake recipes. I think you'll be as delighted as I am to have these on your morning table.

METHOD

1. In a bowl, tear the bread into small pieces before adding in the milk.

2. Using a wooden spoon, beat aggressively until a uniform paste is formed.

3. Add the remaining ingredients, and beat well.

4. Depending on the type of bread used, more milk may be added to create a thinner, pourable batter.

5. Add a few teaspoons of vegetable oil to a frying pan, and heat over medium heat until the oil begins to shimmer.

6. Drop about 3 tablespoons of batter per pancake into the frying pan, shaking it slightly to flatten the pancakes. Cook for roughly 3 minutes on each side. Serve warm.

Sour Cream Cookies

COOKIE • 3 dozen

Prep: 15 minutes
Cook: 15 minutes

½ cup (115g) butter, softened

1 cup (220g) packed dark brown sugar

1 large egg, beaten

½ cup (120g) sour cream

2 cups (280g) all-purpose flour

½ tsp ground nutmeg

2 tsp baking powder

¼ tsp baking soda

¼ tsp salt

If your grandma were to take the form of a cookie, you might become traumatized and quickly reach for emergency services amid a deluge of confused tears. But when I say that these *Sour Cream Cookies* are grandmothers, I mean that they are all the things we cherish about a loving grandma embodied in an unassuming and twee cookie. I describe them as sweet and spiced nubbins of chewy hugs, and although they're most similar to the more dominant snickerdoodle, I'd take these old-world cookies over them any day.

METHOD

1. Preheat the oven to 350°F (180°C).

2. In a large bowl, cream together the butter and brown sugar until fluffy. Beat in the egg and sour cream.

3. In a separate bowl, combine the remaining ingredients before adding to the creamed mixture. Mix well.

4. Drop by level tablespoon or small cookie scoop onto a parchment-lined baking sheet. Bake for 15 minutes.

5. Cool briefly on the baking sheet before carefully transferring to a wire rack to cool completely.

Chocolate Sauerkraut Cake

CAKE • 10-inch Bundt

Prep: 20 minutes
Cook: 50 minutes

CAKE
1 cup (200g) packed sauerkraut (one 16 fl oz jar)

¾ cup (170g) butter, softened

1⅓ cups (265g) granulated sugar

2 large eggs

½ tsp vanilla extract

2¼ cups (315g) all-purpose flour

½ cup (60g) cocoa powder

1½ tsp baking soda

1 cup (235ml) whole milk, scalded and slightly cooled

GANACHE
4oz (113g) bittersweet chocolate

½ cup (120ml) heavy cream

I was left clueless and perplexed at what ailment, occult possession, or rabid fever dream might've led to the first person thinking that sauerkraut belonged anywhere near a dessert, let alone inside chocolate cake. I felt as if I were being played for a fool. And I was a fool—but only for doubting. I have uncovered a few potential reasonings for this unlikely pairing. One firm belief was that a shortage of coconut during wartime led some home bakers to simulate the texture of coconut within their cakes, and thus they reached for sauerkraut. I find this unlikely. Another was that it was an unorthodox manner through which to achieve a moist crumb. This is more plausible. But I have settled on this: that the unique sour and tart nature of sauerkraut manages to perfectly blend and complement the sweet and bitter notes of cocoa. The added moisture and unique crumb are only of additional benefit. What you get after baking this strange gem, is a grand chocolate cake with a wonderful tang that does not make itself known save for its ability to elevate the chocolate to new, unknown heights.

CAKE METHOD

1. Preheat the oven to 350°F (180°C). Grease a 10-inch (25-cm) Bundt pan with butter and dust with flour.

2. Drain, thoroughly rinse, and chop the sauerkraut finely, measuring out 1 packed cup. Set aside.

3. In a large bowl, cream together the butter and sugar until light and fluffy. Beat in the eggs and the vanilla.

4. In a separate bowl, combine the flour, cocoa powder, and baking soda. Fold into the creamed mixture alternately with the scalded milk.

5. Fold in the chopped sauerkraut.

6. Turn into the prepared pan and bake for 45 to 50 minutes, or until a toothpick inserted into the center can be removed cleanly. Cool in the pan for 10 minutes before inverting onto a wire rack to cool completely.

GANACHE METHOD

7. Chop the chocolate into small pieces and place in a heatproof bowl. If using chips, simply place the chips in the heatproof bowl.

8. Scald the heavy cream just below boiling in a small saucepan or in a microwave-safe container. Make sure the cream never boils. Pour this over the chocolate and let sit for 3 minutes.

9. Beat the mixture smooth using a whisk, and once cooled to a thickened consistency, pour over the cooled Bundt cake.

Applesauce Graham Cracker Torte

TORTE • Three 9-inch layers

Prep: 30 minutes
Cook: 48 minutes

TORTE
¾ cup (170g) butter, softened

1½ cup (300g) granulated sugar

1 large egg

Yolks of 4 large eggs

5¼ cups (575g) fine graham cracker crumbs

5 tsp baking powder

1½ tsp ground nutmeg

2 tbsp ground cinnamon

3 cups (750g) unsweetened applesauce

BRANDIED CREAM
2 cups (470ml) heavy cream

½ cup (60g) powdered sugar

1 tsp cream of tartar

¼ tsp ground nutmeg

3 tbsp brandy or sherry

If you've robbed a graham cracker factory and need quickly to disperse of your newfound fortune, this utterly unusual 1940s torte will be very happy to be your accomplice. The flavors of the graham cracker and applesauce are a duo that is begging to be experienced, and this astounding, spongey, and delicately layered torte is the perfect manner in which to do just that. Without any flour at all, this bake is a sophisticated and high-class dessert, and its graceful use of a brandied whipped cream is out of this world.

TORTE METHOD

1. Preheat the oven to 350°F (180°C). Grease three 9-inch (23-cm) cake pans.

2. In a large bowl, cream together the butter and sugar until light and fluffy. Beat in the egg, followed by the egg yolks.

3. In a separate bowl, combine the graham cracker crumbs, baking powder, nutmeg, and cinnamon, whisking to ensure they are well blended. Add to the creamed mixture alternately with the applesauce.

4. Turn into the prepared pans. This batter should be smoothed flat using wet hands because it does not level in the oven.

5. Bake for 43 to 48 minutes, or until a toothpick inserted into the center can be removed cleanly. Cool in pans for 10 minutes before very carefully transferring to a wire rack to cool completely.

BRANDIED CREAM METHOD

6. In the bowl of a stand mixer fitted with a whisk attachment, or a large bowl with which an electric hand mixer is to be used, add the heavy cream, powdered sugar, cream of tartar, and nutmeg.

7. Begin whisking slowly, before increasing to a high speed. Beat in the brandy. Whisk until smooth, stiff peaks are formed, but do not whip beyond this point.

8. Spread a suitable amount of cream evenly atop the first round. Invert the second round atop the filling to form the second layer. Repeat these steps to create the third layer.

9. Spread the remaining cream across the top and sides of the assembled torte. Alternatively, the cream may be added to a piping bag and frosted in this manner. This torte should be stored in the refrigerator when not being served.

> **TIP FROM YESTERYEAR**
> Take care while removing the cakes from the pan, as they can break very easily.

Queen of Puddings

BAKED DESSERT • 1½ quart casserole

Prep: 35 minutes
Cook: 45 minutes

4 cups (175g) soft breadcrumbs, without crust (about 9 slices of sandwich bread)

2 cups (470ml) whole milk

1 large egg

Yolks of 3 large eggs, reserve whites

1 ¼ cup (250g) granulated sugar, divided

1 cup (340g) raspberry preserves

¼ tsp salt

1 tsp vanilla extract

Heavy cream, to drizzle

The British were aware of the *Queen of Puddings* long before the 1940s. It is a traditional UK dessert that has graced tables for centuries. However, its frugal use of premade bread and easily kept preserves led to its meteoric resurgence during the wartime years. Though frugal it may be, it is a warm bowl of absolute patriotic triumph. I have included it in this book, as the "dessert pud" is fairly unknown in the United States. And I believe that the creamy and soft mingling of custard, bright raspberry, and airy meringue might work to turn the attention more to this humble dessert.

METHOD

1. Preheat the oven to 325°F (165°C).

2. Lightly butter a 1 ½ or 2-quart (1.4-1.9L) casserole dish and sprinkle the breadcrumbs evenly on the bottom.

3. In a small saucepan over medium-low heat, scald the milk just below boiling.

4. In a separate bowl, whisk together the egg, egg yolks, and 1 cup (200g) of sugar. Slowly pour in the scalded milk while whisking constantly.

5. Pour the egg and milk mixture over the breadcrumbs. Let stand for about 10 minutes.

6. Place the casserole dish into a larger roasting pan, filling the roasting pan up with enough boiling water to fill at least halfway up the casserole dish. It is best to fill the larger pan with water once on the oven grate, as to not risk spilling hot water.

7. Bake for 30 to 32 minutes, or until the custard has set and a knife inserted into the center can be removed somewhat cleanly. Remove the casserole dish from the oven onto a heatproof surface and raise the oven temperature to 350°F (180°C).

8. Spread the raspberry preserves atop the baked pudding.

9. In the bowl of a stand mixer fitted with a whisk attachment, or in a large bowl with which an electric hand mixer is to be used, beat the reserved egg whites and salt until stiff. Slowly beat in the remaining ¼ cup (50g) of sugar before beating in the vanilla. Beat until glossy, stiff peaks form.

10. Decoratively spread or pipe the meringue over the preserves, taking care not to disturb the layer, and bake at 350°F (180°C), not in the water bath, for another 15 minutes, or until the meringue turns a light golden brown. Serve warm with a drizzle of unwhipped heavy cream.

Peppermint Patties

CONFECTION • 5 dozen

Prep: 1 hour 20 minutes
Cook: None

PATTIES
1 cup (235ml) sweetened
    condensed milk

1½ tsp peppermint extract

5-6 cups (600-720g) powdered
    sugar

CHOCOLATE DIP
4½ cups (765g) semisweet
    chocolate chips

2 tsp of vegetable shortening or
    solid coconut oil, not butter

It is always the best of days when fun times in the kitchen also lead to delicious conclusions, and that is how I feel about making these old-school *Peppermint Patties*. I once thought that the perfectly shaped and delectably minty rounds that we find on store shelves could only be made in a factory, but this 1940s confection showed me that a little effort and simple ingredients could lead to a treat even better than store bought. A homemade, minty fondant of little more than condensed milk and powdered sugar, rolled and cut into neat circles, before being excitingly dipped in a shell of chocolate leads to a refreshing morsel of bliss. I find that these are fun to make with friends or little ones, and regardless of who's in the kitchen I wouldn't blame you if you ate them all.

PATTIES METHOD

1. In a large bowl, combine the sweetened condensed milk and peppermint. Mix well.

2. Gradually mix in the powdered sugar. As the dough becomes stiffer, switch to mixing with your hands. Add enough powdered sugar to make a cohesive, pliable dough that holds its shape well.

3. Place a large sheet of parchment paper down on a work surface, dust the sheet liberally with powdered sugar, and roll the dough to a ¾-inch (2-cm) thickness.

4. Using a small cookie cutter, or the rim of a champagne flute, cut circles roughly 2 inches (5cm) in diameter. Transfer the cut pieces to a tray lined with parchment paper, and refrigerate for at least 1 hour.

CHOCOLATE DIP METHOD

5. Combine the chocolate chips and shortening in a double boiler, stirring once melted until uniform.

6. Using a fork, dip the cold peppermint disks into the chocolate to coat them. Once dipped, scrape the bottom of the fork with a knife to remove any excess chocolate. Place on parchment paper to set at room temperature.

7. Once all the peppermint disks are dipped and the chocolate has set, transfer the patties to an airtight container and store in the refrigerator.

> ### TIP FROM YESTERYEAR
> Be very careful with measuring your peppermint extract! Unlike vanilla extract, peppermint is extremely potent, and just a little excess can become overpowering.

1950s

If the 1900s to the 1940s were incremental steps in changing tastes and desires, then the 1950s were a shell fired from a shotgun. The elderly couldn't clutch their pearls firmly enough to hold back the maelstrom of raucous rock and roll, infectious teen angst, and the outrageous reports of girls across the country now having their thighs visible to the general public. Furthermore, citizens of the 1950s suddenly woke up one morning to a world that was now in color, after centuries of only knowing life in black-and-white. This was surprising to a great number of people.

Innumerable consumer products' advertisements, the golden age of television, and the explosive growth of suburban America meant housewives were ricocheting throughout their larger-than-ever and more well-equipped kitchens with a fire in their eyes equal to the fire in their ovens. If approached too quickly, they'll bludgeon you with a rolling pin, and you'll have deserved it. Because they now had a whole new world of cookery before them, and nothing was to stand in their way.

Bright, spectacular, and easy are the three hallmarks I'd assign to recipes of this era. Cookbooks were filled with copious "cheat" recipes, tips and tricks, and lengthy instructions detailing how to bestow grand desserts on your guests in no time at all. It seemed emphasis was placed not so much on charming and tasty bakes, but on dishes that would dazzle those who beheld them and make you the talk of the bridge party. The Jones's just purchased the newest car on the block after all, so they'll need to be shown up by a firm beatdown in the kitchen, and a new-fangled technicolor cake at your next gathering should do just that.

Here you'll find the voltaic wonders of kitschy 1950s baking: pastel hues, unconventional spectacles, midcentury monarchs, and some fan favorites at their hour of conception.

Melting Moments

COOKIE • 2 dozen

Prep: 45 minutes
Cook: 40 minutes

COOKIE
2 cups (450g) butter, softened

1 cup (120g) powdered sugar

1¾ cups (245g) all-purpose
 flour

1½ cups (200g) cornstarch

½ tsp baking powder

FILLING
½ cup (115g) unsalted butter,
 softened

1¼ cups (150g) powdered sugar

1½ tsp vanilla extract

Clouds aren't typically willing to be eaten, and if they were, they likely wouldn't taste of much good. This old-school, incredible cookie might very well be your next best bet. I don't believe I'm exaggerating when I say that if you've never had *Melting Moments*, you've not lived. They are as if shortbread were to be sanctified and imbued with the heavenly ability to melt in your mouth with the beauty of a million air pockets, all while giving way to the sweet lilt of vanilla buttercream. They are a rich and delicate treat, taking you away from the rigors of life for just one, melting moment.

COOKIE METHOD

1. Preheat the oven to 350°F (180°C).

2. In a large bowl, beat the butter until it lightens, about 5 minutes. Gradually cream in the powdered sugar until creamy and uniform.

3. In a separate bowl, combine the flour, cornstarch, and baking powder. Slowly add this to the creamed mixture, beating well. The mixture should be smooth and creamy, with no visible lumps

4. Chill the dough in the fridge for at least 30 minutes.

5. Using a small cookie scoop or a small spoon, scoop off enough dough to roll 1½-inch (4-cm) balls between hands. This is a wet dough, but it can be done if one accepts messy hands.

6. Place the balls on a parchment-lined baking sheet, allowing 2 inches (5cm) between them. Bake for 18 to 20 minutes, until the edges begin to brown.

7. Let cool for 10 minutes on the baking sheet before transferring to a wire rack. Take care transferring cookies as they are very delicate. Allow the baking sheet to cool between batches.

FILLING METHOD

8. In the bowl of a stand mixer fitted with a paddle attachment, or a large bowl with which an electric hand mixer is to be used, beat the butter until it lightens, about 5 minutes. Gradually beat in the powdered sugar until pale, creamy, and uniform. Beat in the vanilla. Continue to beat for another 3 minutes.

9. Dividing the completely cooled cookies, evenly and carefully spread the filling atop the flat sides of half the cookies. Alternatively, you may place the filling in a piping bag, and pipe a rough tablespoon onto the cookie's centers. Sandwich with the remaining half. Store assembled cookies in an airtight container in a cool environment, or the fridge.

Tomato Soup Cake

CAKE • 9×5-inch loaf

Prep: 30 minutes
Cook: 55 minutes

CAKE
2 tbsp butter, softened

1 cup (200g) granulated sugar

2 cups (280g) all-purpose flour

1 tsp ground cloves

1 tsp ground cinnamon

1 tsp ground nutmeg

¼ tsp salt

1 (10.75oz/305g) can
    condensed tomato soup

1 tsp baking soda

FROSTING
3oz (85g) cream cheese,
    softened

3 tbsp whole milk

3 cups (360g) powdered sugar

1oz (30g) bitter chocolate,
    melted

1 tsp vanilla extract

¼ tsp salt

You might think something has gone terribly awry in a society when condensed tomato soup finds its way into a cake. Perhaps you think of it as an indicator of the beginning of the end, and that we should put a stop to things before it all goes to the pits. I shared this sentiment as I recoiled from the sound of soup entering my batter upon making my first *Tomato Soup Cake*. But the truth is, tomato soup has been the secret ingredient in countless spice cakes even before the 1950s, and the Campbells company jumped on the opportunity and began promoting recipes for soup cakes on their products. The 1950s saw the height of this tomato cake craze, and when paired with a cream cheese frosting, it is unusually and uncomfortably good. Unlike other wild, wacky, and wonderful bakes, I cannot tell you why it works. It is one of the unanswered questions of life. I can only tell you that it does, and you should try it.

CAKE METHOD
1. Preheat the oven to 350°F (180°C). Grease a 9×5-inch (23×13-cm) loaf pan.

2. In a large bowl, cream together the butter and sugar until crumbly.

3. In a separate bowl, combine the flour, cloves, cinnamon, nutmeg, and salt.

4. In a third bowl, combine the condensed soup and baking soda.

5. Working quickly, alternate adding the flour and soup mixtures to the creamed mixture. Mix until barely combined.

6. Turn into the prepared pan and bake for 45 to 55 minutes, or until a toothpick inserted into the center can be removed cleanly. Cool in the pan for 10 minutes before transferring to a wire rack to cool completely.

FROSTING METHOD
7. In the bowl of a stand mixer fitted with a paddle attachment, or in a large bowl with which an electric hand mixer is to be used, beat the cream cheese until smooth. Beat in the milk.

8. Beat in the powdered sugar 2 tablespoons at a time, beating well.

9. Beat in the melted chocolate, vanilla, and salt. Beat until smooth.

10. Frost the completely cooled loaf using a spatula or a piping bag.

Color Vision Cake

LAYER CAKE • Two 9-inch layers

Prep: 30 minutes
Cook: 40 minutes

CAKE

1 cup (225g) butter, softened

1 (6oz/170g) package of cherry Jell-O, divided

1¾ cups (350g) granulated sugar

½ tsp vanilla extract

3 cups (360g) cake flour

3 tsp baking powder (use 2 tsp if baking at or above 5,000 feet)

¾ tsp salt

½ cup (120ml) whole milk

½ cup (115g) sour cream

Whites of 6 large eggs

FROSTING

3 tbsp whole milk, plus more if needed

Remaining Jell-O from cake ingredients

2 cups (450g) unsalted butter, softened

6 cups (720g) powdered sugar, divided

Now you can have your cake "in living color" just like your family's new color television. Chance grandpa's heart condition as he revels in the disabling vibrancy of this bright buttercream and pastel cake. Indeed, this cake is gimmicky, and its inception was undoubtedly just another way for consumer product companies to insert flavored gelatin into all manner of baked goods in midcentury America. But it just so happens marketing isn't always devoid of a fine result: flavoring frostings and batters with the exciting varieties of Jell-O makes for a positively distinctive and idiosyncratic creation, and one that's surprisingly enjoyable, and unmistakably 1950s in its presentation. With the *Color Vision Cake*, you can slice into a piece of yesteryear and celebrate its campy, wonderfully tacky identity.

CAKE METHOD

1. Preheat the oven to 375°F (190°C). Grease two 9-inch (23-cm) cake pans and line the bottoms with parchment paper.

2. In a large bowl, beat the butter until it lightens, about 5 minutes. Beat in 3 tablespoons of the dry Jell-O, and reserve the remainder.

3. Gradually begin to cream in the sugar ¼ cup (50g) at a time. Cream very well until the mixture is light and fluffy. Beat in the vanilla extract.

4. In a separate bowl, sift together the cake flour, baking powder, and salt. Add to the creamed mixture alternately with the milk and sour cream.

5. Beat the egg whites to stiff peaks. Fold into the batter in three additions. Fold well to avoid an uneven cake.

6. Turn into the prepared pans. Bake for 30 to 35 minutes, or until a toothpick inserted into their centers can be removed cleanly. Cool in pans for 10 minutes before transferring to a wire rack. Remove the parchment and cool completely.

FROSTING METHOD

7. Add the milk into a small saucepan on low heat and stir in the remaining Jell-O, stirring consistently. Remove from heat to cool to room temperature.

8. Beat the butter on high speed until it lightens. About 3 minutes. Gradually beat in 4 cups (480g) of powdered sugar, 2 tablespoons at a time. Beat well. With the mixer on, drizzle in the cooled Jell-O mixture.

9. Gradually beat in the remaining 2 cups (240g) of powdered sugar. Beat until pale, creamy, and uniform, about 5 minutes. If the mixture is too stiff to spread, additional milk may be beaten in.

10. Spread the frosting atop the first cake. Invert the second cake atop the frosting to form the second layer. Frost the assembled cake with the remaining frosting.

Boiled Cookies

COOKIE • 3 dozen

Prep: 20 minutes
Cool: 30 minutes

2 cups (400g) granulated sugar

½ cup (120ml) whole milk

½ cup (115g) butter, softened

3 tbsp cocoa powder

3 cups (300g) quick-cooking oats

1 cup (270g) peanut butter

1 tsp vanilla extract

No-bake cookies aren't anything new. The inhabitants of the 1950s figured them out with these boiled cookies, especially once they realized the benefits of quick-cooking oats. Indeed, these cookies have since become known as "No Bakes" in the American Midwest. They were known also as "Preacher Cookies," whereby an unprepared housewife with no treats to offer sees her preacher walking up her lane, and manages to have a full spread of cookies prepared before he reaches her door. Done completely on the stovetop, these fantastic chocolate and peanut butter cookies are like candy in their soft chew and melting sweetness. And you don't even need a bowl!

METHOD

1. In a large saucepan, combine the sugar, milk, butter, and cocoa powder. Stir and bring to a boil. Boil for 1 minute.

2. Remove from heat, and immediately add the oats, peanut butter, and vanilla. Mix until thoroughly combined.

3. Quickly drop from level tablespoon or cookie scoop onto wax paper and let stand at room temperature for at least 30 minutes. Store in an airtight container.

TIP FROM YESTERYEAR
This recipe calls for quick-cooking oats, which are cut finer and soften quicker than other types of oats. The use of rolled oats or "old-fashioned" oats will not work as intended.

Forgotten Cookies

MACAROON • 1 dozen

Prep: 15 minutes
Cook: 4 hours

Whites of 2 large eggs

¼ tsp salt

¾ cup (150g) granulated sugar

1 tsp vanilla extract

1 cup (115g) chopped pecans

1 cup (170g) semisweet
   chocolate chips

As a baker, I find it quite difficult to forget about cookies. I'm driven by some unseen force to bake and then proceed to eat as many of them as my frame allows, and then some. These cookies are forgotten in two senses of the word: they're not in the modern cookie roster any longer, and they're also meant to be left in your oven overnight, as if they were literally forgotten. They are a different type of chocolate chip cookie, in that they are flourless and take the form of a macaroon. The unique method of preparation ensures the perfect, crispy and chewy texture as the meringue cools and dries at its desired slow pace. What you're left with is nothing short of delectable.

METHOD

1. Preheat the oven to 350°F (180°C).

2. In the bowl of a stand mixer fitted with a whisk attachment, or in a large bowl with which an electric hand mixer is to be used, beat the egg whites and salt until stiff.

3. Gradually add the sugar 2 tablespoons at a time before beating in the vanilla. Beat until glossy, stiff peaks are formed.

4. Add the pecans and chocolate, gently folding them into the mixture.

5. Drop by level tablespoons onto a parchment-lined baking sheet. Place in the oven. Once placed, immediately turn off the oven, leaving them to remain overnight, or until the oven is completely cold (at least 4 hours).

Chocolate Mayonnaise Cake

CAKE • 10-inch tube

Prep: 20 minutes
Cook: 45 minutes

CAKE
1½ cups (345g) mayonnaise

1½ cups (300g) granulated sugar

3 cups (420g) all-purpose flour

5 tbsp cocoa powder

¾ tsp salt

2 tsp baking soda

1½ cups (355ml) water

ICING
½ cup (115g) mayonnaise

5 tbsp cocoa powder

1 tbsp whole milk

2 cups (240g) powdered sugar

1 tsp vanilla extract

Mayo is a divisive subject. Many people, like myself, believe it to be a necessity on sandwiches, burgers, and even French fries. Others think it is an abomination and an unholy creation. What is agreed is that it firmly belongs in the realm of savory. Not so with the *Chocolate Mayonnaise Cake*. Whispers of mayo's ability to add tanginess, moisture, and enhanced flavor to cakes began right before the turn of the 1950s, when various US newspaper columns and the National Food Editor's Conference in Chicago in 1949 began to gossip about this secret weapon being used by housewives and restaurants. Those stories turned into recipes in the 1950s, and the craze only took off from there. This cake has made me an even firmer admirer of mayonnaise, as this recipe has become my favorite way to make a chocolate cake. Though it sounds daring, the use of mayo is an economical and easy replacement for oil, eggs, and butter. Its richness is unmatched, and the chocolate mayonnaise frosting somehow manages to be even more chocolatey than chocolate itself. You're bound to find it a winner, and maybe even a perennial standby for family desserts.

CAKE METHOD
1. Preheat the oven to 375°F (190°C). Grease a 10-inch (25-cm) tube pan.

2. In a large bowl, cream together the mayonnaise and sugar.

3. In a separate bowl, combine the flour, cocoa powder, salt, and baking soda. Add to the creamed mixture alternately with the water. Mix until well combined.

4. Turn into the prepared pan, bake for 40 to 45 minutes, or until a toothpick inserted into the center can be removed cleanly. Cool in the pan for 10 minutes before inverting onto a wire rack to cool completely.

ICING METHOD
5. In a double boiler, combine the mayonnaise, cocoa powder, and milk.

6. Gradually add in the powdered sugar, whisking very well until the mixture is smooth and glossy. Remove from heat and stir in the vanilla.

7. Pour and pool the icing on the flat top of the cake, before smoothing with a knife, allowing the icing to drip down the sides. Store the cake in a cool place.

Valentine's Cream Pie

PIE • 9-inch pie

Prep: 30 minutes
Cook: 25 minutes
Cool: 1 hour

PIE
1 single-crust pie pastry
  (page 24)
1 cup (200g) granulated sugar
¼ cup (33g) corn starch
2 large eggs, well beaten
2 cups (470ml) whole milk
½ cup (120ml) maraschino
  cherry juice
½ cup (85g) chopped
  maraschino cherries
½ tsp vanilla extract

WHIPPED CREAM TOPPING
1 cup (235ml) heavy cream
½ cup (60g) powdered sugar
1 tsp cream of tartar
¼ tsp almond extract
Maraschino cherries, for garnish

I can think of nothing better for Valentine's Day than a good old-fashioned cream pie. Secretly, I believe that's what we're all after. After the date is through, and the courting turns to petting, the real goal is a delicious piece of pie on your plate. The 1950s were mad about the maraschino cherry, so much so that it has since become a symbol of the era. This is a custard pie which upholds the glory of that kitschy, neon-red creation as its primary flavor, and it's a winner for it. Sweet, bright, and topped with whipped cream, there has never been anything more appropriate.

PIE METHOD
1. Preheat the oven to 425°F (220°F).

2. Fit your prepared pie crust in a standard 9-inch (23-cm) pan (not a deep pie pan), line with foil or parchment paper, and fill with pie weights, dry rice, or dry beans. Blind bake for 20 minutes, or until the pastry is golden brown. Allow to cool on a wire rack while the filling is prepared.

3. In a saucepan over high heat, combine the sugar, corn starch, beaten eggs, milk, and maraschino cherry juice. Whisking constantly, bring to a boil for 3 minutes, whisking all the while. The mixture should thicken substantially.

4. Remove from heat and mix in the maraschino cherries and vanilla. Pour into the baked pie crust and smooth the top. Place in the refrigerator to cool for one hour.

WHIPPED CREAM TOPPING METHOD
5. In the bowl of a stand mixer fitted with a whisk attachment, or in a large bowl with which an electric hand mixer is to be used, add the heavy cream, powdered sugar, cream of tartar, and almond extract.

6. Begin whisking slowly, before increasing to high speed. Whisk until smooth, stiff peaks are formed, but do not mix beyond this point.

7. Spread the whipped cream generously atop the cooled pie. Top with maraschino cherries. Store covered in the refrigerator until ready to serve.

Kiskadee Fantasy

PIE • 9-inch pie

Prep: 45 minutes
Cook: 1 hour

CRUST
50 saltine crackers, crushed fine
⅓ cup (65g) granulated sugar
½ cup (115g) butter, melted

FILLING
Whites of 2 large eggs
1 tsp white vinegar
¾ cup (150g) granulated sugar
1 tsp vanilla extract

TOPPING
1 (20oz/567g) can crushed
   pineapple
1 cup (235ml) heavy cream
3 tbsp granulated sugar
1 tsp cream of tartar

This pie occupies a special place in my heart, and though my doctor urges that it should be removed, I do not care. Not only is it a 1950s creation of my island home of Bermuda, named after the yellow bodied Kiskadee songbird that is so prevalent on our shores, it is also a recipe that was passed down to me by my father Bruce Hollis. He was the first to make it with me as a younger lad, and I have forever since been enthralled with its simple brilliance. The salty, crisp, buttery crunch of a saltine soda cracker base pairs perfectly with the sweet and chewy meringue. Atop are the bright notes of pineapple and the perfect counterpoint of whipped cream. If summer were a pie, undoubtedly, I would crown it the *Kiskadee Fantasy*.

CRUST METHOD

1. Fine saltine crumbs are best made using a food processor. Combine the finely crushed saltine crumbs, sugar, and melted butter. Mix until uniform, and press evenly into the bottom and sides of a 9-inch (23-cm) pie pan to form a crust.

2. Bake at 400°F (205°C) for 10 minutes, until lightly golden. Let cool on a wire rack while the filling is prepared. Reduce the oven temperature to 325°F (165°C).

FILLING METHOD

3. In the bowl of a stand mixer fitted with a whisk attachment, or in a large bowl with which an electric hand mixer is to be used, beat the egg whites and vinegar to soft peaks, before gradually adding the sugar 2 tablespoons at a time. Beat until stiff peaks are formed. Beat in the vanilla.

4. Turn the meringue into the pie shell, smooth the top, and bake at 325°F (165°C) for 40 to 50 minutes, or until the meringue turns a golden brown. Let cool completely on a wire rack before preparing the topping.

TOPPING METHOD

5. Thoroughly drain the can of crushed pineapple, before laying the pineapple on a bed of paper towels to further pat dry. It is paramount that the pineapple is as dry as possible. Evenly spread the pineapple atop the cooled meringue.

6. In the bowl of a stand mixer fitted with a whisk attachment, or in a large bowl with which an electric hand mixer is to be used, add the heavy cream, sugar, and cream of tartar.

7. Begin whisking slowly, before increasing to high speed. Whip until smooth, stiff peaks are formed, but do not mix beyond this point.

8. Evenly dollop the whipped cream atop the pineapple-laden meringue, spreading carefully so as to not mix the pineapple with the cream. Store in the refrigerator until ready to serve.

Cocomalt Cheesecake

CHEESECAKE • 9-inch springform

Prep: 30 minutes
Cook: 45 minutes
Cool: 2 hours

CRUST
1¼ cups (175g) all-purpose flour

⅓ cup (66g) granulated sugar

⅓ cup (48g) chocolate malted
    milk powder

½ tsp salt

½ cup (115g) butter, melted

CHEESECAKE
2 (8oz/225g) packages cream
    cheese, softened

⅔ cup (132g) granulated sugar

½ cup (125g) cottage cheese,
    at room temperature

2 large eggs, at room
    temperature

⅓ cup (83g) sour cream

½ cup (72g) malted milk
    powder

2 tbsp water

1½ tsp vanilla extract

If a young person were to think of the 1950s, big cars, formal clothes, and rock and roll might come to mind. That, and malted milkshakes. Malt is a flavor many of us like, and which has long been associated with the 1950s. But few know that its flavor comes from not only milk powder, but malted barley and wheat flour. This baked cheesecake capitalizes on that wonderful maltiness and features it in a creamy, soft, and deliciously smooth dessert. Paired with a malted chocolate crust, it is a unique and superb creation.

CRUST METHOD
1. Preheat the oven to 375°F (190°C).

2. In a medium bowl, combine the crust ingredients and mix until a uniform crumb is formed. Press the mixture into the bottom and partway up the sides of a 9-inch (23-cm) springform pan. Bake for 15 minutes.

3. Remove the pan from the oven and let cool on a wire rack. Reduce the oven temperature to 300°F (150°C).

CHEESECAKE METHOD
4. In the bowl of a stand mixer fitted with a paddle attachment, or in a large bowl with which an electric hand mixer is to be used, beat the cream cheese on high speed until smooth.

5. Gradually beat in the granulated sugar until smooth and glossy. Beat in the cottage cheese until smooth.

6. Switching to a low speed, beat in the eggs one at a time.

7. Beat in the sour cream, malted milk powder, water, and vanilla until barely combined.

8. Turn the mixture into the baked crust and bake at 300°F (150°C) for 30 minutes.

9. Turn off the oven, and leave the cheesecake in for another 15 minutes. Remove and let the pan cool on a wire rack to room temperature. Run a sharp knife along the edges of the pan before decoupling, and refrigerate the cheesecake for 2 hours before serving.

Cereal Crunch Nougat Bars

BAR • 9 bars

Prep: 40 minutes
Cool: 3 hours

BAR

36 marshmallows, or 4 ½ cups (225g) mini marshmallows

3 tbsp butter, softened

½ tsp salt

2 tsp vanilla extract

4 cups (120g) Cheerios cereal

½ cup (60g) chopped pecans

1 cup (140g) sweetened shredded coconut

TOPPING

6oz (170g) semisweet chocolate

1 tsp vegetable shortening or solid coconut oil, not butter

In modern times, the Rice Krispies Treat stands as the dominant cereal-based bar confection, utilizing marshmallows and puffed Rice Krispies cereal. However, in years past it was in fierce competition with other cereal contestants like corn flakes and Cheerios for the crown of cereal bars. These *Cereal Crunch Nougat Bars* are one of the old warriors, and they are a marshmallow-bound square of sweet, coconut-y Cheerios, topped expertly with a fine layer of chocolate.

BAR METHOD

1. Line with parchment and lightly grease a 9×9-inch (23×23-cm) baking pan. Melt the marshmallows, butter, and salt in a double boiler. Stir until well combined.

2. Remove from heat and transfer to a large heatproof bowl. Mix in the vanilla.

3. Add in the Cheerios, pecans, and coconut. Stir to ensure everything is well covered.

4. Turn into the prepared pan. Level the mixture in the pan using a piece of wax paper and your hand, or a level glass.

TOPPING METHOD

5. In a double boiler, combine the chocolate and shortening. Stir until the chocolate has melted and the mixture is uniform. Pour over the cereal and level.

6. Set uncovered for 2 to 3 hours at room temperature, or refrigerate for an hour before cutting into square bars of equal size.

TIP FROM YESTERYEAR
Be sure to use vegetable shortening or solid coconut oil for a smooth and silky layer of chocolate. Butter and margarine contain water which can sometimes cause your chocolate to become clumpy or seize!

Cathedral Cookies

CONFECTION • 2 dozen

Prep: 30 minutes
Cool: 5 hours

2 cups (340g) semisweet
   chocolate chips

2 tbsp vegetable shortening or
   solid coconut oil, not butter

½ tsp salt

1 large egg, beaten

1 cup (115g) chopped pecans

3 cups (150g) multicolored mini
   marshmallows

Sweetened shredded coconut,
   or powdered sugar for
   rolling, if desired

No-bake confections are among my favorites. Not only because they're easy, but they're often fun to make and are usually very sweet—something I'm incredibly partial to. These *Cathedral Cookies* are all that; they mimic the stained-glass windows of a cathedral, allowing you to take a bite out of that alluring sanctity without risking sacrilege or a threatening pyre. Chocolate and marshmallows are always a winning combination, and this is perhaps the prettiest marrying of those two around.

METHOD

1. In a double boiler, melt the chocolate chips and the shortening. Add the salt. Stir until well combined. Remove from heat and allow to cool. About 5 minutes.

2. Mix in the beaten egg (if using an uncooked egg is an issue, the mixture may be cooked again in a double boiler for 5 minutes before continuing).

3. Fold in the chopped pecans and marshmallows, ensuring they are evenly coated.

4. Shape into 3 logs, about 2 inches (5cm) in diameter and 8 inches (20cm) long. Roll in the shredded coconut or powdered sugar if desired.

5. Wrap logs in wax paper or aluminum foil and refrigerate overnight, or a minimum of 5 hours. Slice to desired width when ready to serve.

No-Bake

The state of being non-baked has a few benefits, and it's essential if you're employed by any government agency. No-bake goodies are speedy novelties; they reject the complexity of oven temperatures and baking times in favor of simple assembly. Indeed, by leveraging ready-made or store-bought ingredients most of them feel more like arts and crafts than they do cooking. Sometimes, this is precisely the mood we're after when the oven is already occupied, or if the summer heat turns your kitchen into a furnace.

No-bake recipes have been around for centuries, from the 16th-century syllabub, to today's beloved tiramisu. In years long past, they were sometimes denoted as "fireless" recipes, a term I think makes the class sound enticingly magical. However, "fireless" would later be used as a term to describe recipes written for gas and electric ovens as they began to overtake coal and wood-fired stoves and hearths.

So, should you find yourself without an oven or stovetop, simply can't be bothered to use them, or if doing so will put your family in danger of life and limb: this class of baking isn't actually baking at all, and it's for you!

Liquor Balls

CONFECTION • 20 balls

Prep: 30 minutes

½ lb (226g) vanilla wafers, crushed fine

2 tbsp cocoa powder

1 cup (120g) powdered sugar, plus more for rolling

1 cup (115g) finely chopped pecans, or any nuts

2 tbsp corn syrup, or golden syrup

6 tbsp of bourbon, black rum, or any liquor or liqueur

Liquor Balls? I hardly know her. But you probably should, because if you've yet to have a classic bourbon ball or a rum ball you're invariably missing out. Invented in the late 1930s in none other than the bourbon-loving state of Kentucky, the bourbon ball is a bite-size chocolate and bourbon sphere of ecstasy. There have been many variations, some more truffle-like, and some filled with liquor beneath a chocolate shell, but this recipe is the classic cookie-crumb-based, homestyle, no-bake confection. Though bourbon is the traditional liquor of choice for *Liquor Balls,* I'm quite partial to black rum and even hazelnut liqueurs being used in its place. Enjoy the freedom of experimentation as you make these easy, breezy, beauties.

METHOD

1. If one possesses a food processor, all the ingredients can be mixed together in one. Without a food processor, in a large bowl, combine all the ingredients and mix well.

2. Roll by hand into 1- to 2-inch (5-cm) balls.

3. Roll in additional powdered sugar and store in an airtight container.

TIP FROM YESTERYEAR
If you don't have a blender or a food processor to create fine crumbs, you can crush your vanilla wafers by placing them in a bag and rolling them with a rolling pin or wine bottle.

Candle Salad

"SALAD" • Flexible servings

Prep: 5 minutes

Iceberg lettuce

Pineapple, cut into rings

Bananas

Toothpicks

Maraschino cherries

Aerosolized whipped cream

Imagine being seated for dinner as a guest in the 1950s, and peering down at this enticing creation plated before you. Because I do assure you this was a bonafide and earnest table-piece of many midcentury gatherings. How do I eat it? With a knife and fork, or should I tie my hair back? Why does it seem familiar? All good questions and very few answers. What is known is that this fruit salad was erected to mimic a candle, with the banana as the candlestick, the cherry as the flame, and the whipped cream as the wax, all creating a rather excited presentation. It is bar none the fruitiest of fruit salads, and though some of us may instinctively know how to begin on such a meal, do remember to first remove the toothpick holding the cherry.

METHOD

1. Rinse and prepare the iceberg lettuce. One leaf will be used per serving. Place single leaves flat on plates.

2. Place a ring of pineapple, with a center hole cut large enough to snugly accommodate the base of a banana atop the lettuce.

3. Peel bananas and cut one a third of the way up from the stem to allow them to stand as vertical as possible. Place the cut base inside the pineapple ring.

4. Insert toothpicks vertically into the uncut top of the banana, leaving enough exposed to affix a maraschino cherry atop. This will be the candle's "flame."

5. When ready to serve, decoratively apply whipped cream dripping downward from the cherry. This will be the candle "wax."

6. Serve as appetizer table pieces, remembering to remove the toothpicks before eating.

Penguin Icebox Cake

ICEBOX CAKE • 9×13-inch cake

Prep: 30 minutes
Cool: 5 hours

4 cups (940ml) heavy cream

1 cup (120g) powdered sugar

2½ tsp vanilla extract

Roughly 40 chocolate graham crackers, or chocolate wafers

Crushed chocolate graham crackers, chocolate wafers, or shaved chocolate (for garnish)

As speedy as Gonzales, easy as pie, and tasty as ever! Icebox cakes are brilliant. They have been popular ever since the dawn of widespread home refrigeration at the turn of the 1930s. Popularity turned to fanaticism during the mid-1970s, when community cookbooks throughout the United States would be brimming with countless recipes for these chilly creations. Church, women's clubs, and high-school fundraising cookbooks (especially from Wisconsin and Nebraska) would sometimes have entire chapters, fifteen pages deep, dedicated to icebox cakes. I've beheld it myself! The icebox cake that made itself most apparent and carried the most adoration from these homegrown tomes, was a cake made simply from chocolate wafers and whipped cream. And this is what we have here with the *Penguin Icebox Cake!* Smooth and light, interspersed with just the right amount of chocolatey crunch. Make this the night before your gathering, and you'll have one of the easiest fan favorites by your side.

METHOD

1. In the bowl of a stand mixer fitted with a whisk attachment, or in a large bowl with which an electric hand mixer is to be used, add the heavy cream, powdered sugar, and vanilla.

2. Begin whisking slowly, before increasing to a high speed. Whisk until smooth, stiff peaks are formed, but do not whip beyond this point.

3. Evenly spread a thin, base layer of whipped cream over the base of a 9×13-inch (23×33-cm) baking pan or casserole dish. This is only to secure the first layer of graham crackers.

4. Place the first layer of chocolate graham crackers or chocolate wafers atop the whipped cream, cutting them as needed to create a uniform layer.

5. Roughly divide the remaining whipped cream into quarters, spreading the first quarter of the cream atop the first layer of chocolate graham crackers.

6. Place the second layer of graham crackers, before spreading the second layer of whipped cream.

7. Repeat this layering process two more times, ending with a fourth layer of whipped cream.

8. Garnish with crushed chocolate graham crackers or wafers, or shaved chocolate.

9. Cover and refrigerate overnight, or a minimum of 5 hours. Cut and serve cold from the dish.

Magic Ice Cream

SHERBET • 1¼ quarts

Prep: 1 hour 30 minutes
Cool: 2 hours 40 minutes

1 (3oz/85g) package of
   raspberry Jell-O
½ cup (120ml) boiling water
1 cup (200g) granulated sugar
3 cups (700ml) whole milk
1 tsp vanilla extract
1 cup (235ml) heavy cream

If you ask me, all ice cream is magic. We humans are obviously undeserving of such a creation. But to those who occupied the inner cities during the years of the Great Depression, ice cream was simply unattainable. Coveted cream and eggs would've seldom been used for something as extraneous as a frozen treat. Flavored gelatin, which was widely available at the time, did offer a solution. Its thickening abilities could allow for a majority of the cream to be replaced with milk while avoiding the formation of large ice crystals that would usually make such an ice cream too hard. And its structural benefits made the lack of eggs less of a barrier to ice cream making. This *Magic Ice Cream* is a fruit-flavored joy made from quite frugal means, though at the time of the Depression it still would have been an unusually grand treat. Truthfully, it is more of a sherbet than an ice cream. But you can ensure a smoother, softer texture if you agitate the mixture every 40 minutes or so during the initial freezing process.

METHOD

1. In a large bowl, combine the raspberry Jell-O, boiling water, and granulated sugar. Whisk smooth before adding the milk and the vanilla.

2. Refrigerate the Jell-O mixture until it has thickened substantially, but not set. About 50 to 70 minutes. Meanwhile, whip the cream.

3. In the bowl of a stand mixer fitted with a whisk attachment, or a large bowl with which an electric hand mixer is to be used, whip the heavy cream until smooth, stiff peaks are formed, but do not whip beyond this point.

4. Quickly fold the whipped cream into the thickened Jell-O mixture. If the mixture forms clumps, the Jell-O may not be thickened enough and should be returned to the fridge.

5. Once the cream has been folded in, transfer the mixture to a suitable 9×13-inch (23×33-cm) shallow casserole dish. Cover and freeze.

6. For a smoother sherbet, agitate the mixture every 40 minutes by stirring and pulling the freezing edges of the sherbet inward. Repeat 3 to 4 times. Allow at least 30 minutes to partially thaw before serving.

> **TIP FROM YESTERYEAR**
> Though raspberry was the go-to flavor of Jell-O during the Great Depression, feel free to experiment with any flavor!

Coconut Ice

CONFECTION • 2 lbs

Prep: 30 minutes
Cool: 3 hours

1 (14oz/396g) can sweetened condensed milk, divided

2 cups (240g) powdered sugar, divided

2 tsp vanilla extract

Red food coloring

4 cups (340g) unsweetened desiccated coconut, divided

From a young age I've always loved the color pink. This was the first of many signs which would indicate to my parents that I was destined to become a somewhat flamboyant individual. So when I first saw the pink and white hues of these pastel cubes at an elementary school bake sale, young Dylan was to be forevermore enamored with them. *Coconut Ice* is a classic British confection that can be made by even the densest of individuals. With a sweet, toothsome chew of pure coconut flavor, they aim to abate the desires of even the most deprived of coconut dependents. Embrace their cute squareness and jolly coloration, and you'll be better for it.

METHOD

1. Working with two large bowls, place a half can of sweetened condensed milk into each. This is best done with a scale.

2. Thoroughly mix 1 cup of powdered sugar into each bowl.

3. To one bowl, add the vanilla, and to the other bowl, add 2 to 3 drops of red food coloring to make a pink coloration.

4. To each bowl, mix in two cups of the desiccated coconut. Ensure the mixtures are well combined.

5. Thoroughly press the white mixture into the bottom of a parchment-lined 8×8-inch (20×20-cm) or 9×9-inch (23×23-cm) pan, leveling the surface with the bottom of a glass.

6. Thoroughly press the pink mixture atop the white mixture. Leveling as before.

7. Refrigerate overnight, or for a minimum of 3 hours.

8. Remove the set candy from the pan and cut into small cubes.

Ambrosia

"SALAD" • 8 servings

**Prep: 20 minutes
Cool: 1 hour**

2 (11oz/312g) cans mandarin oranges

1 (10oz/283g) jar maraschino cherries

1 (20oz/567g) can crushed pineapple

1⅓ cups (315ml) heavy cream

½ cup (125g) sour cream

1 cup (115g) chopped pecans

2 cups (100g) mini marshmallows

½ cup (70g) sweetened shredded coconut, if desired

The news has come, and it's time for a family potluck. When aunts across the midwestern United States hear this call, they'll surely foam at the mouth and bolt for their recipe cards to whip up a bright, fruity bowl of creamy goodness to thrust upon the buffet after a riveting journey buckled into the passenger seat of the family sedan. This "salad" is infamous. Likely because it hardly meets the requirements to even be considered a salad. But the sweet and fruity song of *Ambrosia* has been sung from as far back the late 19th century in North Carolina, where southern cookbooks would instruct shredded coconut to be layered in tandem with sugar and oranges to give rise to a unique take on fruit salad. This recipe's current, and most well-known, creamy form began to calcify in cooking books around the mid-1910s, where it began to inspire a whole host of American "salads that aren't really salads," most notably the marshmallow salads. *Ambrosia* has since enjoyed tremendous staying power right up into today's kitchens, and although you may cock an eyebrow at this 1950s iteration of bright cherries, coconut, marshmallows, and nuts, you may just find it the food of the gods.

METHOD

1. Drain the mandarin oranges, cherries, and crushed pineapple before laying them atop paper towels to dry.

2. In the bowl of a stand mixer fitted with a whisk attachment, or a large bowl with which an electric hand mixer is to be used, whip the heavy cream until smooth, soft peaks are formed. Do not whip beyond this point.

3. Fold in the sour cream. Then fold in the chopped pecans, marshmallows, and coconut, if using.

4. Fold in the cherries, pineapple, and mandarin oranges.

5. Transfer to a serving bowl, cover, and keep refrigerated.

TIP FROM YESTERYEAR
Be sure to fold the oranges in last, as they're the most liable to break apart.

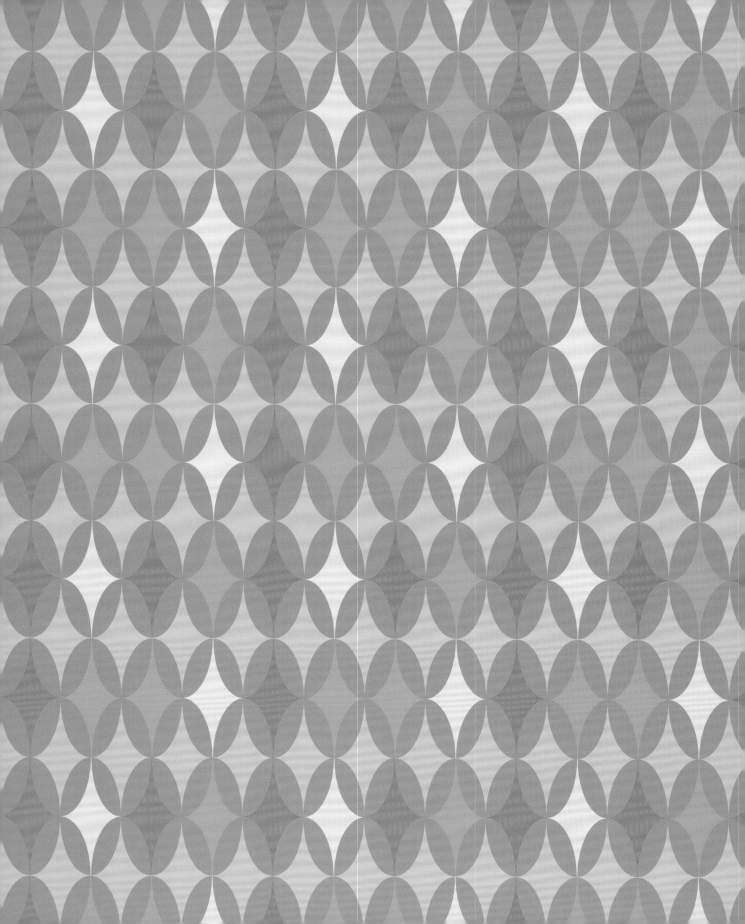

1960s

In many ways, the 1960s were just like the 1950s—they were both decades. But in other ways, the 1960s took on a type of glamorous seriousness that smelled of leather armchairs, ashtrays, and potpourri. Look at any car or kitchen appliance advertisement in the 1950s, compare it to the 1960s, and you'll find that many in the latter try to baroquely appeal to the inner pearl-necklace-wearing, silk-gloved socialite within you.

In the world of baking, this translated to snobbish recipe titles, foreign names for domestic classics, and an enrapturement of gourmet attitudes. 1964's *Ladies' Home Journal Dessert Cookbook* is a fine microcosm of this phenomenon, and was filled with lofty croquembouches, macedoines, and confections which suggested that you should take advantage of your almond orchard and grind eighty pounds of nuts down to a consummate paste before willing a gilded fondant into existence, all before you had to pick up the kids.

Thankfully, there were the community cookbooks of the American Midwest, whose church ladies, local businesses, police departments, and crocheting clubs kept the down-to-earth, simple, and enjoyable side of baking alive and well. The recipes in this section pay homage to the advancements of the everyday baker that took place during the 1960s, taking advantage of a growing variety of ingredients, flavorings, and packaged goods that put yummies in tummies.

Cowboy Cookies

COOKIE • 4 dozen

Prep: 20 minutes
Cook: 1 hour

---

1 cup (120g) unsweetened shredded coconut

1 heaping cup (115g) pecan halves

2 cups (180g) rolled oats

1 cup (225g) butter, softened

1 cup (200g) granulated sugar

1 cup (220g) packed dark brown sugar

2 large eggs

1 tbsp vanilla extract

2 cups (280g) all-purpose flour

1 tsp salt

1 tsp baking soda

2 cups (340g) semisweet chocolate chips

I'm quite partial to cowboys and cowboy culture. I spent eight years at the University of Wyoming in a small town in the American Mountain West called Laramie, where ranching, rodeo, and cowboy culture is alive and well. It was there that I first came across these cookies. You can think of *Cowboy Cookies* as highly optioned, and well-furnished oatmeal cookies with a Costco membership. They take the already scrumptious oatmeal cookie concept and stuff it further with coconut, chocolate chips, and pecans. Combined with notes of brown sugar and vanilla, you're left with a deliciously crispy yet chewy cookie.

METHOD

1. Preheat the oven to 350°F (180°C).

2. On a large baking sheet, lay the coconut, pecans, and oats flat. Toast in the oven for 8 to 10 minutes. Let cool completely on the baking sheet.

3. In a large bowl, cream the butter, sugar, and brown sugar until light and fluffy. Beat in the eggs and vanilla.

4. In a separate bowl, combine the flour, salt, and baking soda. Add to the creamed mixture. Mix well.

5. Chop the toasted and cooled pecans fine.

6. Mix in the toasted coconut, oats, pecans, and chocolate chips.

7. Drop by rounded tablespoons or cookie scoop onto a parchment-lined or greased baking sheet. Bake for 11 to 13 minutes, or until the sides of the cookies begin to brown slightly.

8. Cool briefly on the baking sheet before transferring to a wire rack to cool completely.

TIP FROM YESTERYEAR
Ranger Cookies are a fun variation of Cowboy Cookies. To make these, omit the pecans and chocolate chips, adding 1½ cups (37g) of Rice Krispies (do not toast) in their place. Bake at 350°F (180°C) for 10 to 12 minutes.

Double Chocolate Potato Drops

COOKIE • 4 dozen

Prep: 25 minutes
Cook: 20 minutes

COOKIE
½ cup (115g) butter, softened

1 cup (220g) packed dark
   brown sugar

1 large egg

2 tsp vanilla extract

½ cup (105g) mashed potato,
   cooled

2oz (56g) bitter chocolate,
   melted

1½ cups (210g) all-purpose flour

¾ tsp salt

½ tsp baking soda

¾ cup (180ml) buttermilk

½ cup (55g) chopped walnuts

ICING
1 tbsp butter, softened

1oz (28g) unsweetened
   chocolate

1 cup (120g) powdered sugar

3 tbsp hot water

If you've read through a few of the previous recipes in this book, you'll find that the potato crops up in the quirky, old-school baker's arsenal more than once. It offers moistness, a tight crumb, and a platform which seemingly allows certain flavors to flourish more fully. From my exploration, this concept certainly works in cookies just as it's worked before in cakes and doughnuts. These double chocolate potato drops are my favorite example of the cakey cookie class, and their choco-fiend glaze perfectly complements their rich softness. Their secret lies not only in the potato, but in yesteryear's preference for using melted bitter chocolate over today's more common use of cocoa powder.

COOKIE METHOD
1. Preheat the oven to 375°F (190°C).

2. In a large bowl, cream together the butter and brown sugar until fluffy. Beat in the egg and vanilla.

3. Beat in the mashed potato—ensuring it is cool—and the melted bitter chocolate.

4. In a separate bowl, combine the flour, salt, and baking soda. Add to the creamed mixture alternately with the buttermilk.

5. Fold in the chopped walnuts.

6. Drop by teaspoon or small cookie scoop onto a parchment-lined or greased baking sheet. Bake for 12 to 15 minutes. Let them remain on the baking sheet once removed from the oven.

ICING METHOD
7. In a double boiler, or in a small saucepan over low heat, melt the butter and chocolate.

8. Remove from the heat, and slowly begin whisking in the powdered sugar alternately with the hot water. Whisk smooth.

9. Frost cookies by inverting them into the icing, shimmying, and then removing gently. Transfer to a wire rack to cool completely. Periodically, the icing may need to be whisked to prevent early hardening.

Haystacks

COOKIE • 2 dozen

Prep: 15 minutes
Cool: 1 hour

1 cup (170g) bittersweet
   chocolate chips
1 cup (170g) butterscotch chips
1 (5oz/141g) can chow mein
   noodles
1 cup (130g) salted peanuts

The first recipes for this confection bore the name Chow Mein Cookies in 1963, and when I first came across this confounding title in one of the cookbooks in my collection, the neighbors must've thought I'd completely lost it. I found it absolutely hysterical, especially considering the first ingredient to this cookie was very much canned chow mein noodles. As I was recording my video on the recipe, melting together chocolate and the then newly introduced butterscotch chips (Nestlé released them in 1960), I began to realize that their salty crunch and unique shape might very well lead to an ingenious invention. This was the case, and these chocolate-coated confections, known either as *Haystacks* or Bird Nests today (sometimes with a candy-coated chocolate egg placed atop for Easter) made for a homegrown American treasure. Made in an instant, charming in presentation, and oh-so moreish.

METHOD

1. Melt together the chocolate and butterscotch chips in a double boiler. Stir until uniform.

2. In a large bowl, combine the chow mein noodles and peanuts. Add the melted chocolate mixture and stir quickly to evenly coat them.

3. Using two spoons, dollop roughly 3 tablespoon portions onto wax or parchment paper, forming uneven mounds.

4. Allow at least an hour to set, or if the environment is too warm, they may be refrigerated.

Midnight Mallowmalt Cake

LAYER CAKE • Two 9-inch layers

Prep: 30 minutes
Cook: 35 minutes

CAKE
18 marshmallows, or 2⅓ cups mini marshmallows (¼ lb, 113g)

4oz (113g) bittersweet chocolate

¾ cup (180ml) boiling water

3 large eggs

1¼ cups (250g) granulated sugar

2 tsp vanilla extract

1½ cups (375g) sour cream

2¼ cups (350g) all-purpose flour

¼ cup (36g) malted milk powder

1½ tsp baking soda

1 tsp salt

FROSTING
Whites of 2 large eggs

¾ cup (150g) granulated sugar

⅓ cup (80ml) light corn syrup

1 tbsp white vinegar

1 tsp vanilla extract

Mini marshmallows, for garnish

I once had a man tell me that a chocolate cake is a chocolate cake, and that once you've had one, you've experienced them all. That man is now dead. Chocolate cakes are an entire world waiting to be explored, and this 1960s example is just as badass as its name. With deep chocolate, marshmallow sweetness, and hints of malt and sour cream tartness, all nestled under a snowy blanket of marshmallows and boiled frosting, it is a winner if there's ever been one.

CAKE METHOD

1. Preheat the oven to 350°F (180°C). Grease two 9-inch (23-cm) cake pans.

2. Melt together the marshmallows and the chocolate in a double boiler.

3. Add in the boiling water and beat the mixture smooth. Remove from heat and allow to cool.

4. In a large bowl, beat together the eggs, sugar, and vanilla until thick and foamy. Blend in the sour cream and the cooled chocolate mixture.

5. In a separate bowl, combine the flour, malted milk powder, baking soda, and salt. Gradually add to the wet ingredients. Mix until well combined.

6. Turn into the prepared pans and bake for 25 to 30 minutes, or until a toothpick inserted into the center can be removed cleanly. Cool in the pans for 10 minutes before transferring to a wire rack to cool completely.

FROSTING METHOD

7. In a large bowl that can be placed atop a double boiler, combine the egg whites, sugar, corn syrup, and vinegar.

8. Over boiling water, beat the mixture with an electric hand mixer until it thickens and soft peaks form. Remove from heat and beat in the vanilla.

9. Away from the heat, continue beating until the frosting has cooled and is thick enough to spread onto the cake. This will take some time, about 5 to 6 minutes.

10. Spread a suitable amount of frosting evenly atop the first cake. Invert the second cake atop the filling to form the second layer.

11. Frost the assembled cake with the remaining frosting. Decorate the top of the cake with marshmallows.

> **TIP FROM YESTERYEAR**
> Use the vanilla buttercream frosting recipe on page 25 for an easier frosting option.

Grasshopper Pie

PIE • One 9-inch pie

Prep: 30 minutes
Cook: 10 minutes
Cool: 5 hours

CRUST
1½ cups (170g) finely crushed chocolate wafers, or Oreo cookies, including filling

⅓ cup (66g) granulated sugar

¼ cup (55g) melted butter

PIE
1 (7oz/198g) jar marshmallow creme/fluff

4oz (113g) cream cheese, softened and cubed

¼ cup (60ml) creme de menthe

3 tbsp creme de cacao (white preferred)

3 drops of green food coloring, if desired

2 cups (470ml) heavy cream

⅓ cup (40g) powdered sugar

1 tsp cream of tartar

Shaved chocolate, for garnish

As a single man, I find myself incredibly angry at chocolate's ability to have so many effortless pairings. From hazelnut to strawberries, peanut butter to coffee, and in the case of our pie, mint. Inspired no doubt by the 1918 cocktail of the same name, featuring creme de cacao and creme de menthe, the *Grasshopper Pie* began to appear as a mint-flavored chiffon pie in the early 1950s. During its rise, varying methods of preparation warred for dominance; some featured a minted custard filling, where others used cream cheese, gelatin, or condensed milk. There were graham cracker crusts, coconut meringue crusts, and even traditional pastry crusts. But in the 1960s the smoke cleared, and it was ordained (mostly) that the grasshopper was to be a chocolate-crumbed, marshmallow-based beauty, and thank God for that, because it's a showstopper. This recipe combines marshmallow creme, cream cheese, and freshly whipped cream to create a silky-smooth minty filling perched effortlessly above a chocolate crumb shell.

CRUST METHOD
1. Preheat the oven to 375°F (190°C).

2. Fine wafer or Oreo crumbs are best made using a food processor. In a medium bowl, combine the crust ingredients and mix until a uniform crumb is formed.

3. Press the mixture into the bottom and up the sides of a 9-inch (23-cm) pie pan. Bake for 10 minutes. Remove the pan from the oven and let cool completely on a wire rack.

PIE METHOD
4. In the bowl of a stand mixer fitted with a whisk attachment, or in a large bowl with which an electric hand mixer is to be used, beat the marshmallow creme and cream cheese on high speed until smooth.

5. Reduce the mixer speed to medium low; and with the mixer running, gradually beat in the creme de menthe, creme de cacao, and food coloring, if using. Beat until smooth. Set this mixture aside while you whip the cream.

6. In a clean bowl, using a stand mixer fitted with a whisk attachment, or in a large bowl with which an electric hand mixer is to be used, add the heavy cream, powdered sugar, and cream of tartar. Begin whisking slowly, before increasing to a high speed. Whisk until smooth, stiff peaks are formed.

7. Fold the whipped cream into the marshmallow creme mixture in three additions and turn into the cooled crust. Smooth the top.

8. Cover and refrigerate overnight, or a minimum of 5 hours. Serve cold, garnished with shaved chocolate or crushed chocolate wafers.

Lemon Sponge

BAKED PUDDING • 1½ quart casserole

Prep: 30 minutes
Cook: 1 hour

Yolks of 3 large eggs, reserve whites
1 cup (200g) granulated sugar
Zest of 1 lemon
3 tbsp all-purpose flour
1 cup (235ml) whole milk
Juice of 1 lemon
½ tsp salt

I possess some pretty strong opinions within the world of baking, and one of them is this: traditional soufflés vex me. Sure they may be good, but they are far too posh and pompous. Just as driving around in an exotic car makes you look like a right git, I find serving a soufflé to your friends a bizarre exercise of the ego. I say save it for the restaurant chefs. Now, does part of this avoidance come from the fact that I haven't the skill to make a proper soufflé? Absolutely. Which is why this soft, self-saucing, warm sponge of bliss has become my go-to soufflé-adjacent dessert. Half pudding, half cake, it combines creamy, lemony wonders with a hearty, fluffy crumb.

METHOD

1. Preheat the oven to 325°F (165°C). Lightly grease a 1½ quart (1.4L) casserole dish

2. In a large bowl, lightly whisk together the egg yolks, sugar, and lemon zest.

3. Mix in the flour alternately with the milk.

4. Mix in the lemon juice.

5. In the bowl of a stand mixer fitted with a whisk attachment, or in a large bowl with which an electric hand mixer is to be used, beat the reserved egg whites and salt until stiff. Fold into the first mixture in three additions.

6. Pour the mixture into the prepared dish.

7. Place the casserole dish into a larger roasting pan, filling the roasting pan up with enough boiling water to fill at least halfway up the casserole dish. It is best to fill the larger pan with water once on the oven grate, as to not risk spilling hot water.

8. Bake for 60 to 65 minutes. Serve warm.

TIP FROM YESTERYEAR
Alternatively, these can be baked in standard ramekins (5oz) placed in a hot water bath, for 45 to 50 minutes.

Hello Dollies

BAR • 9×13-inch pan

Prep: 5 minutes
Cook: 30 minutes

½ cup (115g) butter, softened

1½ cups (165g) graham cracker crumbs

1 (14oz/396g) can sweetened condensed milk

1 cup (115g) chopped pecans, or walnuts

1 cup (140g) sweetened shredded coconut

1 cup (170g) semisweet chocolate chips

I'm tempted to give this recipe an award for the laziest cookie in existence, and I say that with all the praise I can muster. Because without a bowl or any mixing utensils at all, you can create a mean, moreish, layered dessert by simply dumping items into your baking pan. Perhaps that is why these are also known as magic cookie bars! Sweet, chewy chocolate and coconut dance with the crunch of a graham cracker crust and any nut of your choosing. Hello, Dolly!

METHOD

1. Preheat the oven to 350°F (180°C).

2. Melt the butter in a 9×13-inch (23×33-cm) nonstick baking pan by placing it in the oven once preheated. Carefully remove, ensuring the butter is evenly dispersed

3. Evenly sprinkle the graham cracker crumbs over the butter, followed by the condensed milk, nuts, coconut, and chocolate chips.

4. Bake for 25 to 30 minutes. Allow to cool completely in the pan before cutting into bars.

Millionaire's Pie

ICEBOX PIE • 9-inch pie

Prep: 20 minutes
Cook: 12 minutes
Cool: 5 hours

CRUST
1½ cups (165g) graham cracker crumbs
¼ cup (50g) granulated sugar
½ cup (115g) melted butter

PIE
1 (14oz/396g) can sweetened condensed milk
1 (20oz/567g) can crushed pineapple, thoroughly drained
1 cup (170g) chopped maraschino cherries, if desired
1 cup (140g) sweetened shredded coconut
Juice of one lemon
1 (8oz/225g)) tub of Cool Whip/whipped topping
½ cup (60g) chopped pecans, for garnish

If you're into large cars, heavy jewelry, and referring to every apparently eligible bachelor and bachelorette as "hot lips," chances are this is the pie for you. Named by midcentury bakers because of its heightened sweetness and downright decadence, the *Millionaire's Pie* is anything but subtle. Pineapple, coconut, and pecans are bejeweled among the creamy filling of the newly invented (1966) Cool Whip whipped topping! If you decide to use maraschino cherries (technically making this a Billionaire's Pie), the pie will take on a brilliantly campy pink hue.

CRUST METHOD
1. Preheat the oven to 375°F (190°C).

2. In a bowl, combine all the crust ingredients and mix until the mixture reaches a wet sand consistency.

3. Evenly press the crumb mixture into a deep 9-inch (23-cm) pie pan, ensuring the sides are well covered.

4. Blind bake for 12 minutes. Remove from the oven and place the pan on a wire rack to cool completely.

PIE METHOD
5. In a large bowl, combine and mix the condensed milk, pineapple, maraschino cherries, coconut, and lemon juice.

6. Pour into the cooled pie shell and refrigerate overnight, or for a minimum of 5 hours. When ready to serve, top with a layer of whipped topping or fresh whipped cream.

7. Garnish with chopped pecans.

TIP FROM YESTERYEAR
Make sure to use the juice of a real lemon, as bottled lemon juice will not cause this pie to thicken.

Avocado Pie

PIE • 9-inch pie

Prep: 25 minutes
Cook: 15 minutes
Cool: 5 hours

CRUST
1½ cups (160g) very fine pretzel crumbs

⅓ cup (66g) granulated sugar

⅔ cup (150g) melted butter

PIE
3 large avocados, skinned and pitted

1 (8oz/226g) package cream cheese, softened

1 (14oz/396g) can sweetened condensed milk

¾ tsp salt

2 tsp grated lime zest

Juice of 2 large limes

Lime wedges, for garnish

Whipped cream, for garnish

Millennials weren't the first generation to go berserk over avocado. The folks of the groovy 1960s realized the fruit's prowess for making a whole host of things taste exceptionally good when they came up with this super easy, super tasty pie. Avocado lovers will be overjoyed with the deep, avocado flavor, lightened and sweetened only slightly by cream cheese and sweetened condensed milk. Pair this with the tang of lime and the salty crunch of a pretzel crust and you've got an unusual winner on your hands.

CRUST METHOD
1. Preheat the oven to 375°F (190°C).

2. Fine pretzel crumbs are best made in a food processor. In a bowl, combine all the crust ingredients and mix until the mixture reaches a wet sand consistency.

3. Evenly press the crumb mixture into a 9-inch (23-cm) pie pan, ensuring the sides are well covered.

4. Blind bake for 15 minutes. Remove from the oven and place the pan on a wire rack to cool completely.

PIE METHOD
5. Place the avocados in the bowl of a stand mixer, or in a large bowl with which an electric hand mixer is to be used, and beat until smooth. Alternatively, the avocado may be forced through a sieve for a smoother texture. Measure out 2 cups (450g).

6. Add the cream cheese and beat smooth. About 5 minutes.

7. Beat in the remaining ingredients. Be sure to use fresh lime juice—the pie will fail to set properly if bottled lime juice is used.

8. Transfer the filling into the completely cooled baked crust, and level the top. Refrigerate overnight, or a minimum of 5 hours.

9. Garnish with lime wedges and unsweetened whipped cream, if desired. Store covered and refrigerated. Consume within 2 days.

Scotcheroos

CONFECTION • 9×13-inch pan

Prep: 30 minutes
Cool: 2 hours

1 cup (235ml) light corn syrup

1 cup (200g) granulated sugar

1 cup (270g) peanut butter

5 cups (130g) Rice Krispies cereal

1 cup (170g) bittersweet chocolate chips

1 cup (170g) butterscotch chips

America's obsession with breakfast cereal is more than a century old. When the manic and dogma-possessed Dr. John Kellogg and his brother, W.K. Kellogg, began devilishly experimenting with grains and corn, forcing their inventions onto patients within Michigan's Battle Creek Sanitarium, the cereal kings introduced the craze which ran from 1896 (the patent for Corn Flakes) right up until today. The Kellogg company is worth speaking on, as its home economics department was the OG inventor of the less-maniacally inclined and globally popular Rice Krispies Treats in 1939. However, in 1965 the same department invented a peer to the Rice Krispies Treats that I believe to be plainly superior. *Scotcheroos* are the puffed rice cereal we love, sweetly bound in a sugary, peanut-buttery chew, topped with a stately layer of chocolate and butterscotch. The combination is very nearly heaven.

METHOD

1. Line a 9×13-inch (23×33-cm) pan with parchment paper.

2. In a large saucepan or nonstick skillet over medium-high heat, combine the corn syrup and sugar. Bring to a boil over medium-high heat, stirring occasionally until all the sugar has dissolved. About 3 minutes.

3. Remove from heat and add in the peanut butter. Stir until uniform.

4. Quickly stir in the cereal, ensuring everything is well coated.

5. Press this mixture into the prepared pan, pack firmly and evenly using the bottom of a glass.

6. In a double boiler, melt together the chocolate and butterscotch chips. Spread in an even layer over the packed cereal.

7. Cool completely in a cool place, or in the refrigerator before cutting into bars.

TIP FROM YESTERYEAR
Be careful, making these can be very messy. Be sure to wear an apron.

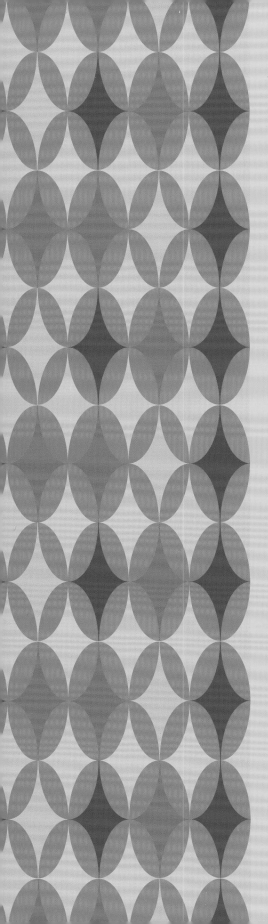

1970s

I've come to call many of the 1970s home baker's recipes "assembly baking." As in this decade, the idea of using ready-made, partially prepared, or "cheat" ingredients came to be common in cookbooks at full force. I'm unsure if everyone was too busy donning their leisure suits and cruising to discos, or if it was just the clever use of traumatizing advertisement jingles, but suddenly homemade was no longer such an important feature in baking.

Boxed cake mixes, canned pie fillings, Cool Whip, and items from the snack aisle made their way into many casual dessert recipes. You didn't tend to make many of the dishes so much as you assembled them. Now in my opinion, there's no sense populating this section with recipes like "box cake mix + canned fruit." I just wanted to give you an overview of what was going on, and with antique stores and garage sales absolutely flooded with 1970's cookbooks, it might be worth your while to experience that particular side of the decade yourself by picking one up.

Instead, this section is the home of youthful experimentation, and not the kind that made me keenly aware of my sexuality. It upholds the inner child attitude of the 1970s by blending pies, embracing potato chips and peanut butter, and shoving cupcakes in ice cream cones. In addition, there are a few assembly recipes like Christmas Crack and The Robert Redford.

Potato Chip Cookies

COOKIE • 2 dozen

Prep: 1 hour 20 minutes
Cook: 15 minutes

¾ cup (170g) butter, softened

¾ cup (165g) packed dark brown sugar

½ cup (100g) granulated sugar

2 large eggs

2 tsp vanilla extract

1 (8oz/230g) bag of ruffled potato chips, crushed (4 cups crushed), divided

2 cups (280g) all-purpose flour

1 tsp baking soda

¼ tsp salt

1½ cups (255g) semisweet chocolate chips

There are salt lovers and sweet tooths in this world. I find myself firmly in the latter category, as you might well expect for a baker. Thus, my brain fizzed and popped at the ridiculous prospect of using an entire bag of salty potato chips within the recipe of the sanctified chocolate-chip cookie. Giving in to the excesses of American culinary inventiveness, my exploration of this concept left me motionless. A party of gooey chocolate, sultry salt, and a crisp, flaky shell made this particular cookie an object of my eternal affection. This was one of the weightier experiments that made me never dismiss outrightly the apparent absurdity of any home-baker's ideas.

METHOD

1. In a large bowl, cream together the butter, brown sugar, and sugar until light and fluffy. Beat in the eggs and vanilla.

2. Mix in half the crushed potato chips.

3. In a separate bowl, combine the flour, baking soda, and salt. Fold this into the creamed mixture, then fold in the chocolate chips.

4. Thoroughly chill the dough in the fridge for at least 1 hour.

5. Crush the remaining potato chips to a finer crumb and set aside.

6. Preheat the oven to 350°F (180°C).

7. Form the dough into rounded tablespoons and roll in the remaining potato chips.

8. Place formed dough on a parchment-lined or greased baking sheet and bake for 11 to 15 minutes, or until the edges of the cookies begin to brown.

Ice Cream Cone Cupcakes

CUPCAKE • 1 dozen

Prep: 20 minutes
Cook: 32 minutes

CUPCAKE
12 flat bottomed ice cream
    cones
1 large egg
½ cup (120ml) vegetable oil
1 cup (200g) granulated sugar
1 tsp vanilla extract
1½ cups (210g) all-purpose flour
⅓ cup (40g) cocoa powder
½ tsp salt
1 tsp baking soda
½ cup (120ml) hot water

FROSTING
1 cup (225g) unsalted butter,
    softened
2½ cups (300g) powdered
    sugar
1½ tsp vanilla extract
2-4 tbsp whole milk, if needed

Thinking outside the box seldom comes to us easily or very often. This is especially true if you are trapped within an actual box. Which is why having metric tons of cookbooks from the past documenting all the countless instances in which thinking outside the box had occurred is such a boon to the baker's armamentarium. One such idea was simply baking a cupcake in an ice cream cone. I find this to be brilliant. Nestled quaintly in their cones (which, no, do not burn during baking), these chocolate cupcakes, topped in ice cream fashion by a simple vanilla buttercream, are begging to be enjoyed during any kid's birthday party or adult's sad, nostalgic longing for times when we were actually happy.

CUPCAKE METHOD

1. Preheat the oven to 350°F (180°C).

2. On a large baking sheet covered with foil, place righted ice cream cones. Make sure your oven rack is in a position which will allow enough clearance.

3. In a large bowl, whisk together the egg, vegetable oil, sugar, and vanilla until smooth.

4. In a separate bowl, combine the flour, cocoa powder, salt, and baking soda. Alternate mixing in the wet ingredients with the hot water.

5. Divide the batter into the 12 ice cream cones, filling them just shy of two-thirds of the way. Bake for 30 to 32 minutes, or until a toothpick inserted into their centers can be removed cleanly. Transfer to a wire rack and allow them to cool completely.

FROSTING METHOD

6. In the bowl of a stand mixer fitted with a paddle attachment, or in a large bowl with which an electric hand mixer is to be used, beat the butter until it lightens. About 5 minutes.

7. Gradually beat in the powdered sugar until pale, creamy, and uniform. Beat in the vanilla. If the mixture is too stiff to pipe, milk may be beaten in a tablespoon at a time. Continue to beat for another 3 minutes.

8. Transfer the buttercream into a piping bag fitted with a nozzle of your choice, and pipe your desired amount of frosting atop the cooled cupcakes to simulate an ice cream cone.

Cold Oven Cake

CAKE • 10-inch Bundt

Prep: 15 minutes
Cook: 1 hour 15 minutes

1½ cups (340g) butter, softened

3 cups (600g) granulated sugar

5 large eggs

1 tsp vanilla extract

1 tsp almond extract

3 cups (420g) all-purpose flour

½ tsp baking powder

1 tsp salt

1 cup (235ml) whole milk, room temperature

Softened butter, for coating the pan

All-purpose flour, for coating the pan

Powdered sugar, for garnish

The first instruction we find when beginning a recipe is often: preheat your oven. It's been drilled into me ever since 2007, when Ms. Anne Coakley, my food and nutrition teacher at Warwick Academy assured me that it was never to be forgotten, lest it be the downfall of one's good cooking. Breaking from convention, however, can be a rewarding experience, and this fantastic example of a pound cake is very willing to prove it to you. By placing your batter in a cold oven and bringing the temperature up from a dead start, this sweet, vanilla-y and almond-y pound cake emerges with an opulent, buttery crumb, blissfully counterpointed by a nice, crisp crust. This has become my go-to pound cake recipe.

METHOD

1. In a large bowl, beat the butter until it lightens, about 5 minutes.

2. Gradually begin to cream in the sugar ¼ cup (50g) at a time. Cream very well until the mixture is light and fluffy. Add the eggs one at a time, beating well after each addition. Mix in the vanilla and almond extracts.

3. In a separate bowl, sift together the flour, baking powder, and salt. Alternate adding this to the creamed mixture with the milk, ensuring the mixture doesn't get too stiff nor too loose during the process.

4. Butter a 10-inch tube or Bundt pan very well before liberally adding flour to coat the interior surface. Tap out any excess.

5. Turn the batter into the pan, and place in a cold oven. Set the temperature to 350°F (180°C), and bake for 60 to 75 minutes, or until a toothpick inserted into the center can be removed cleanly. The individual nature of your oven may vary for this, so be vigilant. Sprinkle on powdered sugar to decorate the cake.

Jell-O Poke Cake

CAKE • 9×13-inch cake

Prep: 20 minutes
Cook: 35 minutes
Cool: 1 hour

CAKE
4 large eggs

¾ cup (180ml) vegetable oil

1½ cups (300g) granulated sugar

2¼ cups (315g) all-purpose flour

½ tsp salt

1 tsp baking powder

½ cup (120ml) whole milk

1 cup (235ml) boiling water

1 (3oz/85g) package of Jell-O, (strawberry, cherry, or raspberry)

WHIPPED CREAM
1 cup (235ml) heavy cream

½ cup (60g) powdered sugar

1 tsp cream of tartar

Should a lofty, sophisticated, and classically trained French pastry chef come across this recipe, they'd likely fall to the floor weeping and decry the downfall of humanity. When did making a perfectly executed laminated pastry or a flawlessly smooth crème patisserie turn into oafishly stabbing a white cake with the handle of a spoon and haphazardly dumping on bright-red liquid Jell-O? Well, it was when home bakers decided to embrace the simplicities they and their families desired—and this philosophy is what this cookbook is all about. The *Jell-O Poke Cake* is distinctly 1970s suburban America: assembling cheap, available pantry items in novel fashions to create sweet, easy desserts. It's a vanilla cake moistened uniquely by flavored gelatin, offering bright pockets of fruitiness beneath a sweet, airy whipped topping. It's as refreshing as it is fun for the kids, and I think you'll agree.

CAKE METHOD
1. Preheat the oven to 350°F (180°C). Grease a 9×13-inch (23×33-cm) pan.

2. In a large bowl, whisk together the eggs, vegetable oil, and sugar until smooth.

3. In a separate bowl, combine the flour, salt, and baking powder. Alternate adding to the first mixture with the milk.

4. Turn into the prepared pan and bake for 30 to 35 minutes, or until a toothpick inserted into the center can be removed cleanly. Place atop a wire rack to cool (in the pan) to room temperature. When cool, poke holes in the cake at 1-inch (2.5-cm) intervals using the handle of a wooden spoon.

5. In a heatproof, pourable vessel, pour the boiling water over the Jell-O and mix until dissolved. Allow the Jell-O mixture to cool to room temperature.

6. When cooled, evenly pour the Jell-O across the surface of the cake. Place in the refrigerator to chill for at least an hour.

WHIPPED CREAM METHOD
7. In the bowl of a stand mixer fitted with a whisk attachment, or in a large bowl with which an electric hand mixer is to be used, add the heavy cream, powdered sugar, and cream of tartar.

8. Begin whisking slowly, before increasing to high speed. Whisk until smooth, stiff peaks are formed, but do not whip beyond this point.

9. Spread the whipped cream atop the cooled cake. Store covered in the refrigerator until ready to serve.

PB King

LAYER CAKE • Three 6-inch layers

Prep: 30 minutes
Cook: 45 minutes

CAKE
½ cup (135g) peanut butter

¼ cup (55g) butter, softened

½ cup (100g) granulated sugar

½ cup (110g) packed dark
   brown sugar

2 large eggs

2 cups (280g) all-purpose flour

1 tsp baking soda

½ tsp baking powder

½ tsp salt

1 tsp ground cinnamon

1 cup (250g) unsweetened
   applesauce

FROSTING
1 cup (270g) peanut butter

1 cup (225g) unsalted butter,
   softened

⅓ cup (45g) cocoa powder

3½ cups (420g) powdered
   sugar

4 tbsp whole milk, plus more if
   needed

I don't think I'll ever be freed of my carnal appetite for peanut butter and chocolate. It'd take death or a hurried lobotomy to end this affliction. However, my symptoms are abated, albeit momentarily, by this absolute unit of a cake. Rich peanut butter flavor in a delicious crumb, covered in the silkiest of chocolate-peanut-butter frosting, the folks of the 1970s were taking no prisoners when they shed light on *the PB King*.

CAKE METHOD

1. Preheat the oven to 350°F (180°C). Grease three 6-inch (15-cm) cake pans.

2. In a large bowl, beat together the peanut butter and butter until uniform. Cream the sugar and brown sugar in gradually, then beat in the eggs.

3. In a separate bowl, combine the flour, baking soda, baking powder, salt, and cinnamon. Add to the creamed mixture alternately with the applesauce.

4. Turn into the prepared pans, and bake for 35 to 45 minutes, or until the tops of the cake are golden brown, and a toothpick inserted into the center can be removed cleanly. Cool in the pans for 10 minutes before transferring to a wire rack to cool completely.

FROSTING METHOD

5. In the bowl of a stand mixer fitted with a paddle attachment, or in a large bowl with which an electric hand mixer is to be used, beat together the peanut butter and butter on high speed until smooth. About 5 minutes.

6. Add in the cocoa powder, before gradually beating in the powdered sugar ¼ cup (30g) at a time.

7. Add in the milk, and beat on high for another 2 minutes. If the mixture is not an easily spreadable consistency, more milk may be added to thin.

8. Spread a generous amount of frosting evenly atop the first cake. Invert the second cake atop the filling to form the second layer. Repeat to assemble the third layer.

9. Frost the assembled cake with the remaining frosting.

The Robert Redford

ICEBOX CAKE • 9×13-inch cake

Prep: 45 minutes
Cook: 15 minutes
Cool: 1 hour

CRUST
1½ cups (210g) all-purpose flour

1 cup (125g) finely chopped pecans

½ cup (100g) granulated sugar

½ cup (115g) butter, melted

FILLING

Layer 1
½ cup (120ml) heavy cream

1 ½ cups (180g) powdered sugar

1 (8oz/226g) package cream cheese, softened and cubed

Layer 2
1 (3.4oz/96g) package chocolate pudding mix

1 (3.4oz/96g) package vanilla pudding mix

2 cups (470ml) whole milk

Layer 3
1 cup (235ml) heavy cream

⅓ cup (40g) powdered sugar

½ tsp cream of tartar

1 tsp vanilla extract

2 tbsp cocoa powder or ½oz (8g) shaved bittersweet chocolate, for garnish

A fiendishly delicious marriage of smooth chocolate and vanilla puddings, cream cheese tang, and satiny whipped cream, all atop a crunchy butter-nut cookie crust makes *The Robert Redford* dessert an utmost dame of 1970s desserts. There's very little consensus or understanding about where this recipe's name originated from. The alternate name of "better than sex cake" gives insight that Robert Redford, a heartthrob at the time, was simply a placeholder for all that is worthy of being lusted after, just like this dessert. Though Robert isn't my type, his namesake cake very much gets my heart racing.

CRUST METHOD
1. Preheat the oven to 375°F (190°C).

2. In a small bowl, combine the crust ingredients and mix until it reaches the consistency of wet sand. Press this into the bottom of a 9×13-inch (23×33-cm) pan.

3. Bake for 15 minutes. Remove from the oven and let cool completely on a wire rack.

FILLING METHOD
4. Prepare layer 1 in the bowl of a stand mixer fitted with a whisk attachment, or a large bowl with which an electric hand mixer is to be used, by whipping the heavy cream and powdered sugar to stiff peaks. While beating, slowly drop in cubes of cream cheese. Beat until the mixture is uniform. Spread this layer evenly atop the cooled crust. Keep chilled.

5. Prepare layer 2 in a separate bowl, by whisking together both pudding mixes and the milk. Once thickened, spread evenly atop layer 1.

6. Prepare layer 3 by again using a stand mixer or an electric hand mixer, combining the heavy cream, powdered sugar, cream of tartar, and vanilla.

7. Begin whisking slowly, before increasing to high speed. Whisk until smooth, stiff peaks are formed, but do not whip beyond this point.

8. Spread the whipped cream evenly atop layer 2. Garnish with cocoa powder or shaved chocolate. Keep covered and refrigerated.

Banana Oatmeal Cookies

COOKIE • 2 dozen

Prep: 15 minutes
Cook: 12 minutes

¾ cup (170g) butter, softened

1 cup (200g) granulated sugar

1 large egg

½ tsp vanilla extract

1 cup (250g) mashed ripe
   bananas

2 cups (180g) rolled oats

1½ cups (210g) all-purpose flour

1 tsp ground cinnamon

½ tsp salt

1 tsp baking soda

½ cup (60g) chopped pecans

I love bananas for many reasons. For one, we grew them at my family's homestead on the island of Bermuda; a homestead that had once been part of a larger banana plantation, tended to by my great-great grandfather Benjamin Clarence Hollis, whom I was named after (that's what the B. stands for). They also taste amazing, grow in their own packaging, and their shape makes me feel things that others who aren't of my particular persuasion likely do not experience. Which is why when I came across this banana-forward piece of baking, which unusually was not a bread, I rushed to my kitchen. Soft, chewy, and sweetly flavored by brown sugar, cinnamon, and banana, these oaty cakey cookies are a loving companion upon your plate.

METHOD

1. Preheat the oven to 400°F (205°C).

2. In a large bowl, cream together the butter and sugar until light and fluffy. Beat in the egg, vanilla, and mashed bananas.

3. In a separate bowl, combine the oats, flour, cinnamon, salt, and baking soda. Fold into the creamed mixture, then fold in the chopped pecans.

4. Drop by rounded tablespoons onto a parchment-lined baking sheet and bake for 11 to 13 minutes. Allow to cool briefly on the sheet before transferring to a wire rack to cool completely.

Impossible Pie

PIE • 9-inch pie

Prep: 10 minutes
Cook: 1 hour, 10 minutes

4 large eggs

1¾ cups (350g) granulated sugar

½ cup (70g) all-purpose flour

1 cup (140g) sweetened shredded coconut

2 cups (470ml) whole milk

¼ cup (55g) butter, melted

Some things are naturally impossible, like perpetual motion or vegan butchers, but this pie purports to be able to form its own soft crust, gooey center, and crispy topping, all by being thrown into a blender and blitzed to high heavens. Impossible? No! Creamy and coconut-y, this custard pie is laziness and inventiveness in perfect harmony. With a dollop of freshly whipped cream or a scoop of vanilla ice cream, its soft bites won me over as I'm sure it will with you.

METHOD

1. Preheat the oven to 350°F (180°C).

2. Combine all the ingredients in a blender, and blend on high speed for 2 minutes.

3. Pour into a standard 9-inch (23-cm) pie pan and bake for 60 to 70 minutes until the top is golden brown. Place the pan on a wire rack to cool completely before refrigerating. Slice and serve cold. Pie will rise in the oven, and fall during cooling.

TIP FROM YESTERYEAR
This pie can be made without a blender, if the eggs are beaten first, and all ingredients are whisked well in a large bowl.

Deep Fried Cookie Dough

FRITTER • 1½ dozen

Prep: 2 hours 15 minutes
Cook: 10 minutes

DOUGH
½ cup (115g) butter, softened

⅓ cup (66g) granulated sugar

⅓ cup (73g) packed light brown sugar

1 large egg

1 tsp vanilla extract

1⅓ cups (185g) all-purpose flour

1 cup (170g) semisweet chocolate chips

BATTER
1¼ cups (175g) all-purpose flour

¼ cup (50g) granulated sugar

1 tsp baking powder

1 cup (235ml) whole milk

1 tbsp vegetable oil

Vegetable oil, peanut oil, or lard for frying

Powdered sugar, for dusting

It's well known that in America they are willing to deep-fry nearly anything that isn't bolted to the earth. Hotdogs, zucchini, onions, cookies, and several species of large bird have all invariably found themselves in the babbling kiddie pool of oil. But in the mid 1970s a baker who seemingly found herself without a working oven, but in company with a ready and willing deep-fryer, decided to put two and two together—and with a crack of lightning and a hysterical laugh, this powerful and delectable creation was born. Or so is my hypothesis. With this recipe, cookie dough is coated in a crispy fried batter, warming, and melting perfectly the sweet hints of vanilla and gooey chocolate within. When dusted with powdered sugar these warm nuggets are a force to be reckoned with.

DOUGH METHOD
1. In a large bowl, cream together the butter, sugar, and brown sugar until light and fluffy. Beat in the egg and vanilla.

2. Thoroughly mix in the flour, followed by the chocolate chips.

3. Using a cookie scoop, or your hands, form smooth, rounded tablespoons of dough (about 1 inch/2.5cm) onto a parchment-lined baking sheet or a large plate. Refrigerate overnight, or at least 2 hours.

BATTER METHOD
4. In a medium bowl, combine the flour, sugar, and baking powder. Slowly whisk in the milk and vegetable oil, until no lumps remain.

5. In a suitable, heavy bottomed pot, add oil or lard to a depth of at least 3 inches (7cm). Bring to a temperature of 365°F (185°C) before frying.

6. Evenly coat the chilled dough balls in batter, before carefully frying for roughly two minutes on each side, or until the balls take on a dark, golden-brown color. Remove and place on a wire rack lined with paper towels.

7. Serve warm, dusted with powdered sugar.

Christmas Crack

CONFECTION • 2 lbs

Prep: 20 minutes
Cook: 10 minutes

40 saltine crackers

1 cup (225g) butter, softened

1 cup (220g) packed light brown sugar

2 cups (340g) semisweet, or milk chocolate chips (one 12oz bag)

Chopped nuts, peppermint candy pieces, M&M's candies, chocolate bar pieces, or sprinkles, for topping

The Drug Enforcement Administration needn't get themselves involved with this stellar and genius confection, for this treat doesn't need the help of illicit substances to compel its beholders to consume copious quantities. I've never before beheld such a perfect meeting of caramel, chocolate, and salty crunch as I did the day I made *Christmas Crack* on December 9, 2021. I remember it vividly, and it has since become my #1 homemade candy. Beginning this recipe by counting and arranging soda crackers in a grid may seem unorthodox, but since the 1970s the making of crack has become a popular yuletide activity for families in the United States. Among other reasons, the name comes from the sound of the final "crack" when splitting the solid sheet into mouth-watering pieces. And, just as stockings and candle-glow punctuate the quiet midwinter home, *Christmas Crack* longs to sit patiently in a glass jar, eager to offer yet another reason for joy during the season.

METHOD

1. Preheat the oven to 350°F (180°C).

2. Line a large baking sheet with heavy-duty aluminum foil. Arrange a grid of saltine crackers in five rows of eight on the baking sheet. The crackers should all be touching.

3. Vertically crease the sides of the aluminum foil to create a dam that borders the crackers.

4. In a medium saucepan over high heat, combine the butter and the brown sugar, stirring occasionally until it reaches a boil.

5. Once the mixture reaches a full boil, boil for 5 minutes without stirring.

6. Carefully pour the mixture evenly over the saltine crackers. The foil dam will prevent the syrup from spilling.

7. Immediately bake for 7 minutes.

8. Remove from the oven and quickly sprinkle the chocolate chips evenly over the hot crackers. Allow to sit for 2 minutes, or until the chips appear glossy, indicating they have melted.

9. Carefully spread the melted chips in a thin, even layer over the crackers.

10. While the chocolate is still hot, sprinkle on any desired toppings. Chopped walnuts or green and red sprinkles are my favorite options to use.

11. Let cool completely, remove foil, and cut into bite-size pieces.

1980s

Imagine for a moment that you are in a mall arcade on a December night in 1985. The dark blue carpet beneath you is punctuated by neon green and pink shapes, and through the plinking, beeping, and plonking, a cohort of white knee socks lifts your gaze to revel in the rows of glinting machines breathing their warm glow into the otherwise dimly lit room. There is a sweet smell in the air, and though it is likely the combination of discarded bubble gum and pizza crusts from the food court, it could also be an ethereal signal to head back home, because after meatloaf and homework, Mom had promised she'd make cookies.

Indeed, the home-baked goods of the 1980s were about as loud as its arcades and shouting television advertisements, breaking from conventions and not giving a damn about why a particular thing tastes good, but just knowing that it does. The recipes were not self-conscious about their common or lowly natures, they were instead proud of them.

If Aunt Lynn's fudge won the county fair with the weight of a cow in sugar, then Aunt Lynn is a girl boss and both her and her fudge should be praised. It didn't matter if it wasn't the proper way, she has a bloody ribbon! This section is the fun side of community baking in the 1980s, the recipes that members of the local PTA bake because they're popular with most of the kids at birthday parties. There's also a few 1980s retro-takes on bakers' classics, and treats whipped up in the time it takes to load a video game.

Monster Cookies

COOKIE • 1 dozen

Prep: 15 minutes
Cook: 15 minutes

½ cup (115g) butter, softened

1 cup (270g) peanut butter

1½ cups (300g) granulated
sugar

1 cup (220g) packed light
brown sugar

3 large eggs

2 tsp vanilla extract

2 tsp baking soda

4½ cups (400g) rolled oats

1 cup (170g) semisweet
chocolate chips

1 cup (210g) M&M's chocolate
candies

1 cup (130g) chopped salted
peanuts, or pecans

Things are big in America, and this rule extends to the size and scope of cookies, too. The colorful, consumerist craze of the 1980s would understandably give rise to a cookie that was full of everything but the kitchen sink, and large enough to warrant two hands to eat. *Monster Cookies* are for those with a craving for all things sweet, salty, and crunchy. Chocolate chips and candies, oats, peanuts, and vanilla are all gathered here to give praise to the vices of the kitchen. And for what reason, precisely, would you refuse?

METHOD

1. Preheat the oven to 350°F (180°C).

2. In a very large bowl, cream together the butter, peanut butter, sugar, and brown sugar until light and fluffy. Add in the eggs, beating well after each addition.

3. Beat in the vanilla and the baking soda.

4. Add in the remaining ingredients, mixing well to ensure everything is evenly dispersed.

5. Drop by ice-cream scoop (3 to 4 tablespoons) onto a parchment-lined baking sheet, allowing at least 2 inches between cookies. Bake for 12 to 15 minutes.

6. Cool briefly on the baking sheet before transferring to a wire rack to cool completely.

TIP FROM YESTERYEAR
For a smaller sized monster cookie, you can drop by rounded tablespoon or use a cookie scoop, baking for 8 to 10 minutes at the same temperature.

Magic Peanut Butter Cookies

COOKIE • 1 dozen

Prep: 5 minutes
Cook: 10 minutes

1 cup (270g) peanut butter
½ cup (100g) granulated sugar
1 large egg

To be frank, this recipe irritated the hell out of me. Before it, I had only known of the traditional peanut butter cookies of flour, butter, leavening, and all the other ingredients that make up a standard cookie. So to be told of a three-ingredient cookie, without flour or any alternative, had me forthrightly dismiss its possibility. But again, knowledge graces us over the years, and I had simply not accrued enough time under my belt to understand the gluten-free joys of these magic, soft, cakey puffs. In the early 1980s this recipe began to crop up in home baking periodicals in the United States as "magic," "instant," or "children's" peanut butter cookies, taking advantage of the well-advertised ubiquity of name brand peanut butters. Later, brands like Kraft would begin printing this very recipe on their peanut butter jars in Canada as "super-easy" peanut butter cookies. The internet would further capitalize on their ease, and blogs would market them as "three ingredient," which is what many know them as today. Made in an instant, simple as can be, and a worthy occupier of the cookie jar—these peanut butter cookies are a home run.

METHOD

1. Preheat the oven to 350°F (180°C).

2. Combine all the ingredients in a bowl and mix well.

3. Drop by level tablespoons onto a parchment-lined baking sheet and bake for 10 minutes.

4. Cool briefly on the baking sheet before transferring to a wire rack to cool completely.

Banana Split Bars

BAR • 9×13-inch pan

Prep: 20 minutes
Cook: 35 minutes

BAR

1 cup (250g) mashed banana,
   (about 2 ripe bananas)

2 large eggs, beaten

1 cup (200g) granulated sugar

1 (8oz/227g) can crushed
   pineapple

1 tsp vanilla extract

2 cups (280g) all-purpose flour

½ tsp baking soda

1 tsp salt

1 tsp ground cinnamon

½ cup (115g) butter, melted

½ cup (85g) chopped
   maraschino cherries

FROSTING

¼ cup (55g) butter, softened

3 tablespoons whole milk

3 cups (360g) powdered sugar

1 tsp vanilla extract

If you've grown tired of brownies and blondies and are feeling fruity, as I often am, these curious and summery bar cookies will offer you a walk on the other side of the street. Sweet, tropical flavors with a hint of cinnamon await beneath a sugary glaze. These chewy bars are something different for the sweet-tooth desires we so often have.

BAR METHOD

1. Preheat the oven to 350°F (180°C). Grease a 9×13-inch (23×33-cm) baking pan.

2. In a large bowl, add the banana, then beat in the eggs, sugar, pineapple and its juice, and the vanilla.

3. In a separate bowl, combine the flour, baking soda, salt, and cinnamon. Add to the first mixture, beating well.

4. Beat in the melted butter, then mix in the maraschino cherries

5. Turn into the prepared pan and bake for 30 to 35 minutes, or until a toothpick inserted into the center can be removed cleanly. Cool in the pan for 10 minutes before transferring to a wire rack to cool completely.

FROSTING METHOD

6. In a saucepan over low heat, combine the butter and milk until melted and uniform. Remove from heat, and slowly whisk in the powdered sugar and vanilla.

7. Spread over the cooled cake. Cut into bars.

Millionaire's Shortbread

BAR • 9×9-inch pan

Prep: 30 minutes
Cook: 45 minutes
Cool: 3 hours

CRUST
1½ cups (210g) all-purpose flour

½ cup (100g) granulated sugar

¾ cup (170g) butter, cold and cubed

FILLING

Layer 1

1 (14oz/396g) can sweetened condensed milk

¾ cup (170g) butter, softened

¼ cup (55g) packed dark brown sugar

¼ cup (60ml) dark corn syrup, maple syrup, or golden syrup

Layer 2

6oz (170g) semisweet chocolate

1 tbsp vegetable shortening or solid coconut oil, not butter

Growing up on a British island with its fair share of Scottish influence had me staunchly believing that shortbread should be left unmolested. I can almost hear my Scotch mathematics teacher from high school shouting "leave 'em be, Hollis!" But who am I to dismiss the probability that layers of sweet caramel and luscious chocolate would take the royal, buttery shortbread to new heights? *Millionaire's Shortbread*, sometimes called millionaire bars, are validation that the concept is a golden one. Adding toppings to shortbread was not new to the 1980s, in fact it was the Scottish themselves who began adding variations and coatings such as nuts and candied peel in the 1800s. The first concrete instance of caramel as an added layer appeared in a 1970s Australian women's periodical, before a chocolate layer began gracing pages in the early 1980s. Before long, "caramel shortbread" and "chocolate shortbread" turned into *Millionaire's Shortbread*, with the ease of the condensed-milk-based caramel hinting at the dessert's decadence. Layers of brilliance await those who make this treat, and it might just make you feel like a millionaire, too.

CRUST METHOD

1. Preheat the oven to 350°F (180°C).

2. In a large bowl, combine the flour, sugar, and butter. Rub the dry ingredients into the butter with your fingers until the mixture is a uniform consistency, like breadcrumbs. Alternatively, you may use a pastry cutter.

3. Firmly press this into the bottom of a parchment-lined 9×9-inch (23×23-cm) pan. Bake for 30 to 35 minutes, or until the shortbread is a golden brown. Let the pan cool on a wire rack.

FILLING METHOD

4. For layer 1, place a saucepan over medium heat, and combine the sweetened condensed milk, butter, brown sugar, and corn syrup. Stir well. Bring to a boil and let cook until the caramel thickens and darkens, about 5 to 7 minutes. Pour caramel over the shortbread layer.

5. For layer 2, in a double boiler combine the chocolate and shortening. Stir until the chocolate has melted and the mixture is uniform. Pour over the caramel layer and level.

6. Let the shortbread set for 2 to 3 hours at room temperature, or refrigerate for an hour before cutting to bars.

Watergate Cake

LAYER CAKE • Two 9-inch layers

Prep: 15 minutes
Cook: 40 minutes

CAKE
1 cup (235ml) vegetable oil

1 cup (235ml) whole milk

1½ cups (300g) granulated sugar

1 (3.4oz/96g) package pistachio flavored instant pudding mix

1 large egg

1 tsp vanilla extract

3 cups (420g) all-purpose flour

1 tsp salt

2 tsp baking powder

½ tsp baking soda

¾ cup (180ml) 7UP, Sprite, or lemon-lime flavored soda

1 cup (115g) chopped pecans

COVER UP FROSTING
1 (8oz/226g) package cream cheese, softened

½ cup (115g) unsalted butter, softened

1 (3.4oz/96g) package pistachio flavored instant pudding mix

5 cups (600g) powdered sugar

2-4 tbsp whole milk, if needed

Roughly 1 cup (140g) sweetened shredded coconut for decoration, if desired

½ cup (60g) chopped pecans for decoration, if desired

Only the Americans would name a bright-green cake after a political scandal resulting in President Richard Nixon's resignation. But the *Watergate Cake* offers more than just comedy, it offers a good dessert. During the scandal in the mid-1970s, swaths of Watergate-named foods cropped up throughout the country, with this specific cake taking on many forms. Some were just boxed white cake mixes dyed green, others were any variety of nut-laden cakes frosted with green-colored icings. All eventually carried the same basic humor: it's a *Watergate Cake* because of the nuts that are in it, with the icing attempting to cover them up. This recipe could have also landed in the 1970s decade of this book, but through my research, it wasn't truly until the turn of the 1980s when community cookbooks, newspaper recipes, and baking aficionados cemented the hallmark ingredients of pistachio pudding, coconut, pecans, and lemon-lime soda. This is the version which thrives even today. Its homemade, moist crumb, flavored by yummy pistachio pudding and lemon-lime zest, is complemented by a distinctively 1980s cream-cheese pudding frosting. Overtly gaudy and loud, it tastes wonderfully electric.

CAKE METHOD
1. Preheat the oven to 350°F (180°C). Grease two 9-inch (23-cm) cake pans.

2. In a large bowl, combine the oil, milk, sugar, pudding mix, egg, and vanilla. Whisk smooth.

3. In a separate bowl, combine the flour, salt, baking powder, and baking soda. Alternate adding this to the oil mixture with the 7UP.

4. Turn into the prepared pans and bake for 35 to 40 minutes, or until a toothpick inserted into the center can be removed cleanly. Cool in pans for 10 minutes before carefully transferring to a wire rack to cool completely.

COVER UP FROSTING METHOD
5. In the bowl of a stand mixer fitted with a paddle attachment, or in a large bowl with which an electric hand mixer is to be used, cream together the cream cheese and butter until smooth and uniform. Add the pudding mix and beat until smooth.

6. Gradually add in the powdered sugar while beating, two tablespoons at a time. Beat until the mixture is smooth and fluffy. Once all the powdered sugar has been added, a small amount of milk may be needed to lighten the texture.

7. When the cakes are cooled, spread a generous amount of frosting evenly atop the first cake. Invert the second cake atop the filling to form the second layer.

8. Frost the assembled cake with the remaining frosting. Decorate the sides of the cake with shredded coconut, and the top with chopped pecans, if desired.

Cream Banana Cake

LAYER CAKE • Two 9-inch layers

**Prep: 20 minutes
Cook: 50 minutes**

CAKE
1 cup (225g) butter, softened

1¾ cups (350g) granulated
   sugar

2 large eggs

3 cups (420g) all-purpose flour

½ tsp salt

½ tsp baking powder

1½ cups (375g) mashed ripe
   bananas (about 3 large
   bananas)

1 cup (250g) sour cream

1 tsp baking soda

FROSTING
Whites of 2 large eggs

1½ cups (300g) granulated
   sugar

1 tsp corn syrup

5 tbsp water

¼ tsp cream of tartar

1 tsp vanilla extract

I generally think there needs to be more fruitiness in the world. Even those who disagree have been at least incidentally inclined toward the fruity side once or twice in their lives, so I see no point in resisting. Too long has vanilla and chocolate held onto the reins, dominating cake flavors from time immemorial. We should allow cakes like this cream banana cake, a 1980s take on a southern American classic, to head the coup. Pillowy, banana-forward, and topped with a venerable layer of satiny 7-minute frosting, this cream queen has become a favorite at my family dinners.

CAKE METHOD

1. Preheat the oven to 350°F (180°C). Grease two 9-inch (23-cm) cake pans.

2. In a large bowl, cream together the butter and sugar until light and fluffy. Beat in the eggs.

3. In a separate bowl, combine the flour, salt, and baking powder. Set aside.

4. In a third bowl, combine the mashed bananas, sour cream, and the baking soda. Stir briefly.

5. Working quickly, alternate adding the flour and banana mixtures to the first mixture. Mix until barely combined.

6. Turn into the prepared pans and bake for 40 to 50 minutes, or until a toothpick inserted into their centers can be removed cleanly. Cool in the pans for 10 minutes before transferring to a wire rack to cool completely.

FROSTING METHOD

7. In a double boiler, mix the egg whites, sugar, corn syrup, water, and cream of tartar.

8. Using an electric hand mixer, begin beating the mixture over the simmering water until stiff peaks are formed, about 7 minutes. If you feel any graininess between the fingers, or if the frosting has not thickened, cook and beat longer.

9. Remove from heat and add the vanilla.

10. Spread a generous amount of frosting evenly atop the first cake. Invert the second cake atop the filling to form the second layer.

11. Frost the assembled cake with the remaining frosting.

The Buster

ICE CREAM CAKE • 9×13-inch cake

Prep: 30 minutes
Cool: 7 hours

CRUST
40 Oreo cookies (460g), crushed fine, do not remove filling (about 4 cups of crumbs)

½ cup (115g) butter, melted

FILLING
Layer 1
2 quarts (1.9L) vanilla ice cream

1½ cups (195g) salted peanuts

Layer 2
½ cup (115g) butter, softened

1½ cups (355ml) evaporated milk

2 cups (240g) powdered sugar

¼ tsp salt

1 cup (170g) semisweet chocolate chips

1½ tsp vanilla extract

There aren't enough ways to consume ice cream; it is, after all, the world's favorite dessert. The home bakers of the United States knew this when they attempted to replicate American food chain Dairy Queen's Buster Bar in the 1980s. In doing so, they created more than just a copycat, they created what I consider the ultimate ice cream cake. Atop a delectably crunchy chocolate cookie base sits creamy vanilla (or any flavor) ice cream dotted with the salty crumble of peanuts and covered in a smooth, gooey, chocolatey veil. It is a dessert experience that will have your inner child clawing for more

CRUST METHOD

1. Fine Oreo crumbs are best made by putting whole Oreos through a food processor. In a medium bowl, combine the crust ingredients and mix until a uniform crumb is formed.

2. Press the mixture into the bottom of a 9×13-inch (23×33-cm) baking pan or casserole dish. Place in the refrigerator for at least 1 hour before continuing.

FILLING METHOD

3. Prepare layer 1 by first softening the ice cream, allowing it to thaw for 20 to 30 minutes before blending, or beating it smooth in a bowl.

4. Evenly spread the softened ice cream over the crust, before sprinkling an even layer of peanuts over the ice cream. Place in the freezer.

5. Prepare layer 2, in a large saucepan over medium heat, by combining the butter and evaporated milk. Once the butter has melted, whisk in the powdered sugar and salt.

6. Add in the chocolate chips, stirring until all have melted.

7. Bring the mixture to a boil and boil for 8 minutes, stirring and scraping the bottom constantly. The mixture will bubble up greatly.

8. Remove from the heat, stir in the vanilla, and allow to cool for 5 minutes.

9. Remove the pan from the freezer, and pour the chocolate sauce over the ice cream layer, and level. Cover and return to the freezer overnight or for a minimum of 6 hours. Cut into squares and serve from the pan.

PB&J Cheesecake

CHEESECAKE • 9-inch springform

Prep: 30 minutes
Cool: 5 hours

CRUST
1½ cups (165g) graham cracker crumbs

¼ cup (50g) granulated sugar

½ cup (115g) melted butter

CHEESECAKE
3 (8oz/226g) packages cream cheese, softened

½ cup (125g) sour cream

1 cup (270g) peanut butter

1 cup (235ml) heavy cream

½ cup (60g) powdered sugar

1 cup (320g) grape jelly, divided

1 cup (130g) chopped salted peanuts, for topping

SAUCE
½ cup (135g) peanut butter

2 tbsp honey

5 tbsp water

The 1980s were a time of celebrated youth. It was the dawn of video gaming, glowing roller-skating rinks, shopping mall hangouts, and frizzy hair. This cheesecake from this fabulous decade captures the sweetness of youth in the flavors of peanut butter and jelly. Historically, cheesecakes were stodgy, baked affairs. But as the years rolled by, the "no-bake" class began to take the spotlight in the home kitchen, allowing far more inventiveness and experimentation with a variety of flavors. A sweet and silky peanut butter filling is elevated by the crunch of a graham cracker crust, and a heavenly drizzle of grape jelly seals the deal as a rewardingly merry trip down memory lane.

CRUST METHOD
1. Preheat the oven to 375°F (190°C).

2. In a medium bowl, combine the crust ingredients and mix until a uniform crumb is formed. Press the mixture into the bottom, and partway up the sides of a 9-inch (23-cm) springform pan. Bake for 15 minutes. Remove the pan from the oven and let cool completely on a wire rack.

CHEESECAKE METHOD
3. In the bowl of a stand mixer fitted with a paddle attachment, or in a large bowl with which an electric hand mixer is to be used, beat together the cream cheese, sour cream, and peanut butter on medium speed until smooth and uniform. About 5 minutes. Set aside.

4. In a separate bowl, again using a stand mixer or an electric hand mixer, switch to a whisk attachment and whip the heavy cream and powdered sugar to smooth, stiff peaks, but do not whip beyond this point.

5. Fold the whipped cream into the peanut butter mixture in three additions, folding until uniform.

6. Spread ⅔ cup (210g) of grape jelly evenly over the cooled crust, before turning the cheesecake mixture atop. Smooth top, then spread the remaining ⅓ cup (106g) of jelly over the top. Sprinkle chopped peanuts evenly.

7. Refrigerate overnight, or a minimum of 5 hours. Gently run a sharp knife along the edges of the springform pan before decoupling and serving.

SAUCE METHOD
8. In a microwave-safe bowl, or in a small saucepan over low heat, stir together all the sauce ingredients and heat until a pourable consistency is reached. Decoratively drizzle over top the cheesecake before refrigerating, or serve with cut slices.

Velveeta Fudge

CONFECTION • 3 lbs

Prep: 5 minutes
Cook: 10 minutes
Cool: 4 hours

1 cup (225g) butter, softened
½ lb (225g) Velveeta cheese
½ cup (60g) cocoa powder
1 tsp salt
2 lbs (910g) powdered sugar,
    about 7½ cups
2 tsp vanilla extract
1 cup (115g) chopped nuts,
    if desired

I often worry about the mental constitution of some of the recipe writers I come across in my bizarre cookbook collection. When I see things like Velveeta processed cheese mixed with chocolate, I can only assume it's a manifestation of a larger medical syndrome crying out for help, and I feel the need to dial for professional intervention. Only to realize that what's stricken them has certainly already claimed their lives, and all that's left of them is a sad and discombobulated marring of tortured thoughts upon a page. This recipe, however, is one of those special psychiatric symptoms. The creamy, rich, and perfectly salty processed cheese somehow bonds with deep cocoa flavors in ways previously unknown to man. *Velveeta Fudge* is a novel, easy, and rich no-bake fudge that does not belong in our universe, and its existence is likely causing a cosmic instability that thankfully has not yet consumed us.

METHOD

1. In a large saucepan over medium heat, combine the butter and Velveeta until fully melted. Then stir in the cocoa powder and salt until no dry lumps remain. The mixture will look separated.

2. Gradually mix in the powdered sugar. Stir and then beat very well as the mixture thickens.

3. Remove from heat and mix in the vanilla and nuts, if using.

4. Slide onto a parchment-lined 9×13-inch (23×33-cm) pan. Cool to room temperature before transferring to the fridge. Cut into small squares. This fudge is best stored in the fridge and should be cooled for a minimum of four hours.

Worst of the Worst

Just under half of the recipes that I try on my TikTok aren't good. And within that half lay some truly revolting abominations. These creations are the kind that make you ponder the sobriety of the recipe developer, grasp fully the sadistic tendencies of mankind, and ask whether or not certain combinations of ingredients may indeed conjure a portal to hell.

The worst of the worst are almost impressive in how far removed they are from the realm of reality, let alone appetizing. Some of these recipes forced me into a hiatus, or incapacitated me in ways I didn't know were possible. So naturally, I asked myself whether or not it was worth translating them and including them in this book.

I resolved to do so, since the bad experiences of what I do play such a big part in my overall journey of exploring cooking past, and not including them would ignore the fact that some bonafide, published recipes are simply bad—horrendous even.

Proceed into this section with caution, lest you find yourself spouseless or beneath an overturned dining table after serving such a dish like the ones that follow.

Jellied Meatloaf

GELATIN MOLD • 6 ramekins

Prep: 1 hour 20 minutes
Cook: 15 minutes
Cool: Overnight

1 lb (450g) ground beef

1 package/1 tbsp unflavored gelatin

1 cup (235ml) water

1 medium onion, peeled and minced

1 medium stalk of celery, chopped fine

1 tsp salt

1 tsp black pepper

2 cups (470ml) beef stock

½ cup (75g) chopped pimiento peppers

Even the uninitiated individual knows that the more sinister side of old-world cooking undoubtedly dabbled in the dark arts of gelatin. Everything from fruit, vegetables, poultry, and seafood found themselves frozen in time within the jiggling confines of a cold, jellied casket. This was especially the case in the 1930s and the decades surrounding it, when the extravagance of owning the novel home refrigerator was a mark of success, and thus gelatin manufacturers took to advertising recipes to cash in on hosts' desires to impress their guests. Gelatin molds required refrigeration, and thus to be served one was an indicator of the server's wealth. The dark, dank, cold bowels of gelatin companies' test kitchens were places of horrific experimentation, and on one stormy night in 1931, a crazed chef devised his plan: the warm and wholesome meatloaf should instead be frigidly solidified in a jellied beef stock mold, and served bleakly in individual rounds of shame.

METHOD

1. In a skillet or saucepan over medium-high heat, brown the ground beef for 8 to 10 minutes. Stir and break the ground beef into small pieces as it cooks. Drain off any grease and set aside.

2. In a separate, large bowl, soften the gelatin in the water. Set aside.

3. In a pot or saucepan over high heat, briefly cook the onion, celery, salt, and pepper, before adding the chicken stock and boiling for 3 minutes.

4. Strain the hot stock into the gelatin mixture. Stir well.

5. Refrigerate mixture until it thickens but does not set completely (about 40 minutes to an hour). Add in the ground beef and pimiento peppers.

6. Pour into individual serving molds, ramekins, or a loaf pan and refrigerate overnight.

7. To unmold the gelatin, place the vessel in a bath of warm water (not allowing any water to touch the gelatin) for 10 to 20 seconds before inverting onto a serving dish. Failing this, run a thin, sharp knife along the sides and attempt again. Serve cold on a bed of lettuce.

SpaghettiOs Jell-O Ring

GELATIN MOLD • 9-inch Bundt

Prep: 15 minutes
Cook: 15 minutes
Cool: 5 hours

½ cup (120ml) condensed tomato soup

½ cup (120ml) water, divided

2 packages/2 tbsp unflavored gelatin

2 (15.8oz/448g) cans of SpaghettiOs

1 (4.6oz/130g) can of Vienna sausages, or cocktail sausages

Mayonnaise, for serving

Picture a smartly dressed person sitting at a table in the 1960s with a particular problem. They love tomato sauce and the little rounds of cute pasta that float and mingle within it, but they cannot figure out how to slice it or eat it with a knife and fork. This is vexing—it is simply too liquidy, and despite sleepless nights and their best efforts, the sauce and miniature pasta insults them as it continues to slip past the tines of their fork. This is utterly unacceptable. A plan is drawn up to solidify this foolish soupiness and create a structure that will yield to the superiority of human inventiveness. It is a sight to behold: a rounded, gelatin mold of canned pasta, cold and clammy as a corpse, with the added benefit of a center pocket to hold slimy fingers of Vienna sausages, offering a sick addition as they finally become able to slice and chew their pasta sauce.

METHOD

1. In a saucepan over medium heat, combine the condensed tomato soup and ¼ cup (60ml) water. Bring to a simmer, but not a full boil. Meanwhile, mix the gelatin into the remaining cold water. Grease a 9-inch (23-cm) Bundt pan, 1½ quart (1.4L) mold, or similarly sized vessel.

2. Once the soup mixture has simmered, remove from heat and mix in the gelatin mixture.

3. Mix in the SpaghettiOs.

4. Pour into the prepared pan, and refrigerate overnight, or for a minimum of 5 hours.

5. To unmold the gelatin, place the vessel in a bath of warm water (not allowing any water to touch the gelatin) for 10 to 20 seconds before inverting onto a serving dish. Failing this, run a thin, sharp knife along the sides and attempt again. Serve cold with Vienna sausages in the center of the circular mold. Serve with mayonnaise.

Roughage Loaf

QUICKBREAD • 9×5-inch loaf

Prep: 10 minutes
Cook: 55 minutes

1 cup (105g) wheat germ

½ cup (120ml) hot water

1 cup (235ml) buttermilk

1 cup (235ml) molasses

1 large egg, well beaten

1 cup (140g) graham flour,
    or whole wheat flour

½ tsp ground cloves

½ tsp salt

1 tsp baking soda

½ cup (80g) chopped prunes

Dietary fiber is an important part of our everyday nutrition. It keeps our tummies happy as much as it keeps us regular. But whoever invented this roughage loaf at the turn of the 20th century must've had a digestive system equatable to Niagara Falls, and was in need of a military-grade solution to regulate the onslaught of their deluge with unwavering force. This quickbread is perfect should you ever want to experience the joys of childbirth on a whim. A whole cup of pure wheat germ will expertly paralyze your gut, forming a mass worthy of statehood before the sweet lull of prunes stimulate your body into flight, and initiates a purge as delicate and gentle as a traffic collision.

METHOD

1. Preheat the oven to 350°F (180°C). Grease a 9×5-inch (23×13-cm) loaf pan.

2. In a large bowl, combine the wheat germ, hot water, buttermilk, and molasses. Allow to hydrate for 10 minutes. Beat the egg into the wheat germ mixture.

3. In a separate bowl, combine the graham flour, cloves, salt, and baking soda. Beat this into the wheat germ mixture.

4. Mix in the chopped prunes.

5. Turn into the prepared pan and bake at for 45 to 55 minutes, or until a toothpick inserted into the center can be removed cleanly.

6. Cool in the pan for 10 minutes before transferring to a wire rack to cool completely.

Prune Whip Pie

PIE • 9-inch pie

Prep: 30 minutes
Cook: 35 minutes

1½ cups (250g) chopped prunes
½ cup (120ml) water
½ cup (100g) granulated sugar
1 cup (115g) chopped walnuts
Whites of 3 large eggs
½ tsp salt
1 single-crust pie pastry,
    (page 24)

I do not think it is a stretch to say that most of you reading this are averse to the prune. This is primarily because you are alive. But those before us did not share this viewpoint; to them the prune was as worthy a fruit as any to be enjoyed, and enjoy it they did in the 1920s in a strikingly diverse number of ways. Prune whip began as a standalone meal: prunes would be soaked and revived by boiling, before being folded into a meringue which could either be left unbaked or baked. What resulted was a fluffy mound of sickly sweet white and purple goo, and they were happy to have it. This pie would later take the concept and turn it into a sliceable piece of laxative, gently browned in the oven and presented to you in a steaming triangle of neat, revolting glory.

METHOD

1. Preheat the oven to 350°F (180°C).

2. Place the chopped prunes in a small bowl and pour enough boiling water to cover them. Allow them to steep for 10 minutes.

3. Drain the water from the prunes, and place them in a medium saucepan with ½ cup (120ml) of fresh water.

4. Over medium-high heat, stir in the sugar and bring the mixture to a boil, stirring constantly. Boil for 5 minutes, or until most of the water has evaporated.

5. Remove from heat and stir in the walnuts. Allow the mixture to cool completely.

6. Meanwhile, in the bowl of a stand mixer fitted with a whisk attachment, or in a large bowl with which an electric hand mixer is to be used, beat the egg whites and salt to stiff peaks.

7. Fold in the completely cooled prune mixture.

8. Fit your prepared pie crust in a standard 9-inch (23-cm) pan (not deep pie pan), and turn in the prune-laden meringue.

9. Bake for 30 to 35 minutes, or until the top of the meringue is a golden brown.

Pickle Cheesecake

CHEESECAKE • 9-inch pie

Prep: 25 minutes
Cook: 55 minutes

CRUST
1½ cups (160g) very fine pretzel crumbs

⅓ cup (66g) granulated sugar

⅔ cup (150g) butter, melted

CHEESECAKE
2 (8oz/226g) packages cream cheese, softened

4oz (113g) goat cheese, softened

1 cup (250g) sour cream

¼ cup (60ml) dill pickle juice

1 large egg

¼ cup (25g) grated Parmesan cheese

1 tbsp onion powder

1 tsp red pepper flakes

½ tsp salt

1 cup (150g) chopped dill pickle, drained

Upon my first encounter with this 1970s foe on August 23, 2021, I called it the devil quiche. It is a haphazard mosh pit of cheeses, savory spices, and, inexplicably, dill pickles. Having the gall to be baked in a lovely pretzel crust, it attempts to put lipstick on a pig and call itself a savory, appetizer cheesecake worthy of your charcuterie spread. It is more worthy of a dumpster so that you might avoid its vinegary brine of poisoned dairy and spicy nightmares. Should you find this enjoyable, I suggest that you immediately note your location and forward it to the relevant authorities.

CRUST METHOD
1. Preheat the oven to 375°F (190°C).

2. Fine pretzel crumbs are best made in a food processor. In a bowl, combine all the crust ingredients and mix until the mixture reaches a wet sand consistency.

3. Evenly press the crumb mixture into a 9-inch (23-cm) pie pan, ensuring the sides are well covered.

4. Par-bake for 10 minutes. Remove from the oven and place the pan on a wire rack to cool completely. Lower the oven temperature to 350°F (180°C) as you prepare the pie.

CHEESECAKE METHOD
5. In the bowl of a stand mixer fitted with a paddle attachment, or in a large bowl with which an electric hand mixer is to be used, beat the cream cheese until smooth and uniform.

6. Beat in the goat cheese, followed by the sour cream, pickle juice, and egg. Beat very well.

7. Beat in the Parmesan, onion powder, pepper flakes, and salt.

8. Fold in the chopped pickles.

9. Turn into the pie crust, and bake for 45 minutes, or until the top of the pie turns a light, golden brown. Serve warm as an appetizer.

Conclusion

The experience of putting together *Baking Yesteryear* for you was a pleasure unmatched. Not only as an opportunity to breathe new life into dishes that once held the hearts of those in the old world, but as a celebration of the fact that while the cakes might change, the joys of baking remain timeless.

As I sat in my kitchen, surrounded by piles of old cookbooks, comparing ingredients, referencing recipes, and experimenting and adapting them to create the best versions of these dishes, it dawned on me that each recipe writer was, in their own way, simply trying to share something that made them feel good. It didn't matter if it was a plain cookie or a three-tiered torte; or if it was from 1901 or 1988—the sharing of a dessert and how to make it was an exercise in sharing happiness.

I realized then why I was having so much fun writing this book—I was thrilled to simply have the chance to share what makes me happy, and in turn, the joys and the delights of our bygone bakers. I sincerely hope that *Baking Yesteryear* serves you well, and offers you the opportunity to taste just a sliver of the past's ingenuity, and the magic that I feel comes with it.

From my kitchen to yours,

Dylan

Acknowledgments

It is undeniably the case that *Baking Yesteryear* would not exist if it weren't for the kindness, generosity, and support of millions of strangers on the internet. So foremostly, I sincerely thank anyone and everyone who has ever watched, shared, commented, or otherwise engaged with my content. It was you who seem to have decided that my loud and obnoxious short videos were something of merit. From TikTok to Tumblr, and Instagram to YouTube, I'm very grateful for you all.

It is also the case that this book could not exist in such a wonderful state if it weren't for the expertise of my editor, Alexander Rigby. From inception to completion, he was able to translate my anarchic and nonstandard passion for baking into the book before you.

I must also thank my family, especially my mom Shawn and my dad Bruce for raising me in a way that allowed me to be proud of my idiosyncrasies, and thus made me eager to share them with the world.

To Jake, my landlord and friend. Without my apartment and its iconic kitchen, I'm not sure that me and the hobby of baking would have ever met.

To Dr. Michael Griffith, Dr. Ben Markley, Dr. Andy Wheelock, Maria Almendares, Dr. Scott Turpen, Dr. Theresa Bogard, and Ed Breazeale: I thank you for all the opportunities, life lessons, and second chances you gave me while I studied at the University of Wyoming. You each allowed me the time I needed to set myself right.

Thank you to all the fans and viewers who mailed their old cookbooks to me over the years. Without you, I would not have had the extensive collection required to fully realize *Baking Yesteryear*.

To my friend Ben, thanks, you're dumb. :)

Thank you to friends Parker, Aidan, Alie, Tony, Adrien, Nate, Kailey, Shantell, Kate, Jane, Hays, Kelly, Bradley, and Kelton.

And to DK and Penguin Random House, thank you for giving me the opportunity to become an author. I will be forever grateful.

About the Author

B. Dylan Hollis is a social media personality who has tasked himself with baking and tasting unusual recipes from bygone years. Born and raised on the island of Bermuda, he later attended college at the University of Wyoming to further a career as a jazz pianist and arranger. He stumbled into both baking and social media fame at once in 2020, when quarantine boredom led him to film an investigation of an old cookbook he had collected from an estate sale. Hundreds of recipes later, Dylan now entertains millions across TikTok, YouTube, and Instagram with his unique style and fast jokes.

Index

#

1900s, 27–45
    Cornflake Macaroons, 31
    Cream Spice Cake, 35
    Election Cake, 39
    "fireless cookery," 27
    Food for the Gods, 32
    Hermits, 45
    Hot Cross Buns, 43–44
    Pecan Dainties, 28
    Pioneer Brownies, 40
    Sandtorte, 36

1910s, 47–65
    Admiral's Gingerbread, 53
    ANZAC Biscuits, 58
    Carrot Pie, 62
    Chocolate Potato Cake, 54
    Divinity, 65
    The Lady Baltimore, 57
    Pork Cake, 50
    Rice Pudding, 59
    Starchies, 49

1920s, 67–83
    Anadama Bread, 82
    Blackberry Jam Cake, 77
    Continental Johnny Cake, 78
    Dutch Apple Cake, 74
    Hedgehogs, 70
    Maple-Squash Gems, 72
    Poorman's Pie, 73
    Ricciarelli, 69
    Unemployment Pudding, 81

1930s, 97–115
    Baked Apples, 112
    Banana Marlow, 115
    Icebox Pinwheels, 99
    Mock Apple Pie, 108
    Peanut Butter Bread, 103
    Potato Candy, 113
    Potato Doughnuts, 111
    Rocks, 100
    Wacky Cake, 104
    Whipped Cream Cake, 107

1940s, 117–135
    Applesauce Graham-Cracker Torte, 131
    Chocolate Sauerkraut Cake, 128
    Dream Bars, 120
    Leftover Bread Pancakes, 126
    Oatmeal Honey Bread, 123
    Peanut Butter Styrofoams, 119
    Peppermint Patties, 135
    Queen of Puddings, 132
    Sour Cream Cookies, 127

1950s, 137–155
    Boiled Cookies, 144
    Cathedral Cookies, 155
    Cereal Crunch Nougat Bars, 153
    Chocolate Mayonnaise Cake, 147
    Cocomalt Cheesecake, 152

Color Vision Cake, 143
    Forgotten Cookies, 145
    Kiskadee Fantasy, 151
    Melting Moments, 139
    Tomato Soup Cake, 140
    Valentine's Cream Pie, 148

1960s, 171–189
    Avocado Pie, 186
    Cowboy Cookies, 173
    Double Chocolate Potato Drops, 174
    Grasshopper Pie, 181
    Haystacks, 177
    Hello Dollies, 183
    Lemon Sponge, 182
    Midnight Mallowmalt Cake, 178
    Millionaire's Pie, 185
    Ranger Cookies, 173
    Scotcheroos, 189

1970s, 191–211
    Banana Oatmeal Cookies, 206
    Christmas Crack, 210
    Cold Oven Cake, 197
    Deep Fried Cookie Dough, 209
    Ice Cream Cone Cupcakes, 194
    Impossible Pie, 207
    Jell-O Poke Cake, 201
    PB King, 202
    Potato Chip Cookies, 193
    The Robert Redford, 205

1980s, 213–231

Banana Split Bars, 219

The Buster, 227

Cream Banana Cake, 224

Magic Peanut Butter
Cookies, 216

Millionaire's Shortbread,
220

Monster Cookies, 215

PB&J Cheesecake, 228

Velveeta Fudge, 231

Watergate Cake, 223

A

Admiral's Gingerbread, 53

Ambrosia, 168

Anadama Bread, 82

ANZAC Biscuits, 58

Applesauce Graham Cracker
Torte, 22, 131

"assembly baking," 191

Avocado Pie, 186

B

bad recipes. See worst of the
worst

Baked Apples, 112

baked custard, Lemon
Sponge, 182

baked pudding
Date Soufflé, 87
Rice Pudding, 59

baking powder, 20

baking soda, 20

baking tray, 19

baking ware, 19

Banana Marlow, 115

Banana Oatmeal Cookies, 206

Banana Split Bars, 219

bars. See also cookies
Banana Split Bars, 219
Date Bars, 88
Dream Bars, 120
Hello Dollies, 183
magic cookie bars, 183
Millionaire's Shortbread,
220
Pioneer Brownies, 40

beat, definition of, 16

"better than sex cake," 205

Biscoitos de Maizena, 49

biscuits, Rocks, 100

Blackberry Jam Cake, 77

Boiled Cookies, 144

Boston School of Cookery, 27

breads
biscuits, Rocks, 100
cornbread, Continental
Johnny Cake, 78
muffins, Maple-Squash
Gems, 72
quickbreads
Admiral's Gingerbread,
53
Date Nut Loaf, 94
Oatmeal Honey Bread,
123
Peanut Butter Bread,
103
Pork Cake, 50
Roughage Loaf, 238
yeast breads
Anadama Bread, 82
Hot Cross Buns, 43–44

brownies, Pioneer Brownies,
40

brown sugar, 20

Bundt cake, Whipped Cream
Cake, 107

bundt pans, 19

The Buster, 22, 227

Buster Bar (Dairy Queen), 227

butter, 20

C

cakes
"better than sex cake," 205
Blackberry Jam Cake, 77
bundt, Whipped Cream
Cake, 107
Chocolate Mayonnaise
Cake, 147
Chocolate Potato Cake, 54
Chocolate Sauerkraut
Cake, 128
Cold Oven Cake, 197
Cream Banana Cake, 224
icebox cakes
The Buster, 227
PB&J Cheesecake, 228
Penguin Icebox Cake,
162
The Robert Redford,
205
Jell-O Poke Cake, 201
The Lady Baltimore, 57
layer cakes
Color Vision Cake, 143
Cream Spice Cake, 35
Midnight Mallowmalt
Cake, 178
PB King, 202
Sandtorte, 36
Tomato Soup Cake, 140
upside-down cake, Dutch
Apple Cake, 74
Wacky Cake, 104
Watergate Cake, 223
Whipped Cream Cake,
107

yeast-risen, Election Cake, 39

cake tins, 19

Candle Salad, 160

Carrot Pie, 62

cast iron skillet, 78

Cathedral Cookies, 155

Cereal Crunch Nougat Bars, 153

cheesecakes
    Cocomalt Cheesecake, 152
    PB&J Cheesecake, 228
    Pickle Cheesecake, 240

Chocolate Mayonnaise Cake, 147

Chocolate Potato Cake, 22, 54

Chocolate Sauerkraut Cake, 128

Chow Mein Cookies, 177

Christmas Crack, 22, 191, 210

Clarkson, Kelly, 50

Coakley, Anne, 197

Cocomalt Cheesecake, 152

Coconut Ice, 167

Cold Oven Cake, 197

Color Vision Cake, 143

confectioner's sugar, 20

confections
    Cathedral Cookies, 155
    Cereal Crunch Nougat Bars, 153
    Christmas Crack, 210
    Coconut Ice, 167
    Divinity, 65
    Liquor Balls, 159
    Peppermint Patties, 135
    Potato Candy, 113
    Scotcheroos, 189
    Velveeta Fudge, 231

Continental Johnny Cake, 78

cookies. See also bars; macaroons
    ANZAC Biscuits, 58
    Banana Oatmeal Cookies, 206
    Boiled Cookies, 144
    Cathedral Cookies, 155
    Chow Mein Cookies, 177
    Cowboy Cookies, 173
    Double Chocolate Potato Drops, 174
    Haystacks, 177
    Hedgehogs, 70
    Hermits, 45
    Icebox Pinwheels, 99
    Magic Peanut Butter Cookies, 216
    Melting Moments, 139
    Monster Cookies, 215
    no-bake, 144, 155
    Potato Chip Cookies, 193
    Ranger Cookies, 173
    Sour Cream Cookies, 127
    Starchies, 49

cookie sheet, 91

cornbread, Continental Johnny Cake, 78

Cornflake Macaroons, 31

COVID-19 pandemic, 12

Cowboy Cookies, 173

cream, definition of, 16

Cream Banana Cake, 224

Cream Spice Cake, 35

cupcakes, Ice Cream Cone Cupcakes, 194

custard, baked, Lemon Sponge, 182

D

Dairy Queen, 227

dates, 85–95
    Date Bars, 88
    Date Macaroons, 93
    Date Nut Loaf, 94
    Date Soufflé, 87

Deep Fried Cookie Dough, 209

devil quiche, 240

dietary fiber, 238

Divinity, 65

double boiler, 16

Double Chocolate Potato Drops, 174

doughnuts, Potato Doughnuts, 111

Dream Bars, 120

dried fruit, 32

Dutch Apple Cake, 74

E

Edebiri, Ayo, 50

eggs, 20

Election Cake, 39

electric hand mixer, 19

F

Farmer, Fannie Merritt, 27, 40

favorites, 22
    Applesauce Graham Cracker Torte, 131
    The Buster, 227
    Chocolate Potato Cake, 54
    Christmas Crack, 191, 210
    Food for the Gods, 32
    Haystacks, 177
    Kiskadee Fantasy, 151

Ricciarelli, 69
Whipped Cream Cake, 107
"fireless cookery," 27
"fireless" recipes, 157
flour, 20
fold, definition of, 16
Food for the Gods, 22, 32
Forgotten Cookies, 145
fried dough, Potato Doughnuts, 111
fritter, Deep Fried Cookie Dough, 209
frosting, Vanilla Buttercream Frosting, 25

G

gelatin molds, 235, 236
golden syrup, 58
Grasshopper Pie, 181
Great Depression, 67, 73, 81, 97, 103, 104, 108, 112, 163

H

Haystacks, 22, 177
Hedgehogs, 70
Hello Dollies, 183
Hermits, 45
Hollis, Benjamin Clarence, 206
Hollis, Bruce, 151
Hoosier Pie, 73
Hot Cross Buns, 43–44

I

icebox cakes
The Buster, 227
PB&J Cheesecake, 228

Penguin Icebox Cake, 162
The Robert Redford, 205
icebox pie, Millionaire's Pie, 185
Icebox Pinwheels, 99
ice cream. See also sherbet
Banana Marlow, 115
Ice Cream Cone Cupcakes, 194
icing sugar, 20
Impossible Pie, 207
ingredients, 20
baking powder, 20
baking soda, 20
brown sugar, 20
butter, 20
confectioner's sugar, 20
eggs, 20
flour, 20
icing sugar, 20
milk, 20
powdered sugar, 20
salt, 20
sugar, 20

J

Jellied Meatloaf, 235
Jell-O Poke Cake, 201 Jell-O, 143, 201

K

Kellogg, John Harvey, 31, 189
Kellogg, W.K., 189
Kiskadee Fantasy, 22, 151
kitchen scale, 19

L

Ladies' Home Journal Dessert Cookbook (1964), 171
The Lady Baltimore, 57
layer cakes
Color Vision Cake, 143
Cream Spice Cake, 35
Leftover Bread Pancakes, 126
Lemon Sponge, 182
Leno, Jay, 50
Liquor Balls, 159
loaf pan, 19

M

macaroons. See also cookies
Cornflake Macaroons, 31
Date Macaroons, 93
Forgotten Cookies, 145
Peanut Butter Styrofoams, 119
Pecan Dainties, 28
Ricciarelli, 69
magic cookie bars, 183
Magic Ice Cream, 163
Magic Peanut Butter Cookies, 216
Maple-Squash Gems, 72
marlow, Banana Marlow, 115
measuring cups, 19
measuring spoons, 19
Melting Moments, 139
Midnight Mallowmalt Cake, 178
milk, 20
Millionaire's Pie, 185
Millionaire's Shortbread, 220
misc, Baked Apples, 112
mixing bowls, 19

Mock Apple Pie, 108

molds

    Jellied Meatloaf, 235

    Spaghetti-O Jell-O Ring, 236

Monster Cookies, 215

muffins, Maple-Squash Gems, 72

N

National Food Editor's Conference (1949), 147

New Book of Cookery: Eight-hundred and Sixty Recipes Covering the Whole Range of Cookery, A (1912), 47

Nixon, Richard, 223

no-bake recipes, 157–169

    Ambrosia, 168

    Candle Salad, 160

    Coconut Ice, 167

    Liquor Balls, 159

    Magic Ice Cream, 163

    Penguin Icebox Cake, 162

"No Bakes," 144

O

Oatmeal Honey Bread, 123

OG cookies, 45

P

pancakes, Leftover Bread Pancakes, 126

parchment paper, 19

PB&J Cheesecake, 228

PB King, 202

peaks, definition of, 16

Peanut Butter Bread, 103

Peanut Butter Styrofoams, 119

Pecan Dainties, 28

Penguin Icebox Cake, 162

Pennsylvania Dutch, 74

Peppermint Patties, 135

Pickle Cheesecake, 240

Pie Crust, 24

pie pans, 19

pies

    Avocado Pie, 186

    Carrot Pie, 62

    Grasshopper Pie, 181

    icebox pie, Millionaire's Pie, 185

    Impossible Pie, 207

    Kiskadee Fantasy, 151

    Mock Apple Pie, 108

    Pickle Cheesecake, 240

    Poorman's Pie, 73

    Prune Whip Pie, 239

    Valentine's Cream Pie, 148

Pioneer Brownies, 40

Poorman's Pie, 73

Pork Cake, 12, 50

Pork Cake, 50

Potato Candy, 113

Potato Chip Cookies, 193

Potato Doughnuts, 111

pots, 19

Pouding Chomeur, Unemployment Pudding, 81

powdered sugar, 20

"Preacher's Cookies," 144

Priscilla Cook Book for Everyday Housekeepers, The (1913), 47

Prune Whip Pie, 239

pudding

    baked

        Date Soufflé, 87

        Rice Pudding, 59

        Queen of Puddings, 132

        Unemployment Pudding, 81

Q

Queen of Puddings, 132

quickbreads

    Admiral's Gingerbread, 53

    Date Nut Loaf, 94

    Oatmeal Honey Bread, 123

    Peanut Butter Bread, 103

    Pork Cake, 50

    Roughage Loaf, 238

R

ramekins, 81, 182, 235

Ranger Cookies, 173

Ricciarelli, 22, 69

Rice Krispies Treats, 153, 189

Rice Pudding, 59

Riverside County Fair and National Date Festival, 85

The Robert Redford, 191, 205

Rocks, 100

Roughage Loaf, 238

rubber spatula, 19

S

"salads"

    Ambrosia, 168

    Candle Salad, 160

salt, 20

salted butter, 20

Sandtorte, 36

saucepans, 19

Scotcheroos, 189

Sequilhos, 49

sherbet, Magic Ice Cream, 163

sieve, 19

skillets, 19

sling, 10

soft peaks, definition of, 16

Sour Cream Cookies, 127

SpaghettiOs Jell-O Ring, 236

springform pan, 32

stand mixer, 19

Starchies, 49

stiff peaks, definition of, 16

sugar, 20

Sugar Cream Pie, 73

Swingle, Water T., 85

T

terms, 16
    beat, 16
    cream, 16
    double boiler, 16
    fold, 16
    peaks, 16
    soft peaks, 16
    stiff peaks, 16

TikTok, 12, 50, 233

Tomato Soup Cake, 140

tortes
    Applesauce Graham Cracker Torte, 131
    Food for the Gods, 32

tube pans, 19

U

Unemployment Pudding, 81

unsalted butter, 20

upside-down cake, Dutch Apple Cake, 74

utensils, 19
    baking ware, 19
    electric hand mixer, 19
    kitchen scale, 19
    measuring cups, 19
    measuring spoons, 19
    mixing bowls, 19
    parchment paper, 19
    pots, 19
    rubber spatula, 19
    saucepans, 19
    sieve, 19
    skillets, 19
    stand mixer, 19
    whisk, 19
    wooden spoon, 19

V

Valentine's Cream Pie, 148

Vanilla Buttercream Frosting, 25

Velveeta Fudge, 231

W–X

Wacky Cake, 104

Warwick Academy, 197

Watergate Cake, 223

Whipped Cream Cake, 22, 107

whisk, 19

whole milk, 20

wooden spoon, 19

World War II, 97, 100, 107

worst of the worst, 233–241
    Jellied Meatloaf, 235
    Pickle Cheesecake, 240
    Prune Whip Pie, 239
    Roughage Loaf, 238
    SpaghettiOs Jell-O Ring, 236

Y–Z

yeast breads
    Anadama Bread, 82
    Hot Cross Buns, 43–44

yeast-risen cake, Election Cake, 39